Salmon

Animal
Series editor: Jonathan Burt

Already published

Salmon

Peter Coates

REAKTION BOOKS

Published by
REAKTION BOOKS LTD
33 Great Sutton Street
London EC1V 0DX, UK
www.reaktionbooks.co.uk

First published 2006

Printed and bound in Singapore by CS Graphics

British Library Cataloguing in Publication Data
Coates, Peter A., 1957–
    Salmon. – (Animal)
    1. Salmon 2. Salmon fisheries – History
    I.Title
    597.5'6

    ISBN-13: 978 1 86189 295 9
    ISBN-10: 1 86189 295 0

Contents

Introduction

One of the most striking stories we have taken from the lives of our fellow creatures is the one about the salmon's last journey to do its 'natural duty' (to quote Izaak Walton).[1] Whereas many creatures reproduce season after season for as long as they live once they reach sexual maturity, the salmon's entire life is geared toward a single act of reproduction in the frigid place of its birth that marks the culmination of its existence. Salmon fighting their way upstream to spawn is one of nature's most fantastic spectacles. Observing it on the Bol'shaya river on Siberia's Kamchatka Peninsula, a Russian ichthyologist compared a school of migrating salmon a kilometre long and a hundred metres wide to 'the noise of boiling water splashing in a gigantic cauldron'.[2]

The salmon's stamina is also famous. A Briton reported in the 1840s that it could cover 24 feet (7.3 metres) per second in relatively calm lake waters. At 86,400 feet (26.3 kilometres) an hour, he calculated that a salmon could circumnavigate the globe in just a few weeks![3] After expending their final spurts of energy, their frayed and decaying bodies collapse and they die within weeks – sometimes days. (A 2003 TV commercial for the UK's best-selling brand of confectionery showed salmon struggling upstream; the slogan read 'Remember you are not a salmon. Have a break. Have a KitKat' – and even appeared on the wrapping paper. Catching the mood, Cheltenham Borough Council staged a 'dead salmon day', supported by 700 free KitKat chocolate bars, on 10 June 2003; staggered breaks of 10–20 minutes were designed to allow demoralized staff who often felt like hapless salmon fighting the current to 'reflect on how they can improve their working life'.)[4] Salmon also undergo remarkable physiological changes to prepare themselves for saltwater life and to re-equip themselves for a return to freshwater some years later, after thousands of miles of ocean roaming,

Inspired by its remarkable life cycle, we have selected the salmon as a symbol of indomitable fortitude and endurance, self-sacrifice, loyalty to place, untamed wildness, irrevocable fulfilment of destiny and the powerful intimacy between life and death. We routinely describe its journey home as a pilgrimage or an epic. (The salmon features as a symbol of wondrous voyaging and inter-galactic roving in a posthumous collection of writings by the author of *The Hitchhiker's Guide to the Galaxy*.)[5] Moreover, by general consensus, the fish is unmatched in beauty among its peers. 'The form of a salmon, fresh run from the sea', remarked a nineteenth-century British angler, '*is* faultless.'[6] This awareness of beauty is heightened by its brevity, the onset of spawning quickly converting a gorgeous, shapely fish into something 'lean and ugly' (to quote the German naturalist Georg Wilhelm Steller).[7] Fish tend to lack the qualities of beauty, dignity and grandeur that endear certain mammalian members of the animal kingdom to us. But we have elevated the salmon to the regal ranks of the tiger, the lion and the stag. The king of kings, the chinook salmon of the Pacific (also known as king salmon), can weigh as much as 56 kilograms and measure 1.5 metres. Over short distances, it can accelerate faster than a Ferrari.

The kingly salmon's habits have puzzled observers for centuries. As Thomas Fuller remarked in the Herefordshire chapter of his renowned county-by-county survey of England's prominent people, wonders, buildings and natural commodities (1662), the salmon presented 'a double riddle in Nature: first, for its invisible feeding, no man alive having ever found any meat in the maw thereof. Secondly, for its strange leaping (or flying rather).'[8] Whether or not the salmon eats on re-entering freshwater, how it can surmount obstacles and how high it can jump are just a few of the fish's curiosities that have engrossed the attention of natural historians, ichthyologists and anglers since medieval times. Chapter One (Biological Salmon, or the salmon as fish) examines the natural and evolutionary history of the various salmon species pieced together by those who have striven to understand a 'strange and splendid organism with a strange and wonderful life-history'.[9] The salmon's homing instinct is one of the natural world's greatest wonders and one of the most enduring of biological mysteries.

Yet the fish offers much more than a scientific challenge. Relations between salmon and people in the northern hemisphere are close, extensive and long-standing; in fact, we co-evolved with them. Chapter Two (Edible Salmon, or the salmon as food) looks at the most basic form of contact that we (and many other creatures) have had with them: as consumers of their nourishing flesh. Entire communities have been embedded in salmon, giving rise to the notion of 'salmon nation' and 'salmon people'. For tribal populations sharing its freshwater range on North America's west coast, the salmon occupied the same position as the buffalo in the lives of the Indians of the Great Plains.

Since the Middle Ages, however, this local food, the basis of subsistence economies, has become a lucrative commodity within an increasingly global economy. And, unlike many other natural resources, the available amount has actually expanded.

'Even under Socialism', admitted the leading writer on the British Left in the 1890s, 'there might not be enough salmon and pineapple for all'.[10] Yet subsequent developments in the making of fish confounded Robert Blatchford's notion of a finite resource. Thirty years ago, fresh salmon was a luxury item in European cuisine. Now it is one of the most widely available of fishes thanks to the aquaculture boom. It is difficult to make a case for salmon as another fish that changed the world (a reference to Mark Kurlansky's *Cod: A Biography of the Fish that Changed the World*). For many in North America and western Europe, though, farmed salmon is the new cod. A much coveted fish traditionally associated with privilege is now one of the cheapest on the fishmonger's slab.

Salmon is a controversial as well as widespread dish, though, and a highly paradoxical fish. News bulletins and front-page stories announce the latest scientific studies that advise us to limit our consumption of farmed salmon on health and ecological grounds. Celebrated for centuries by enamoured anglers as the noblest of fish, a heroic symbol of unfettered freedom, the salmon is now just as likely to be deplored as the ignoble product of the aquatic equivalent of battery farming. (The recent British brouhaha peaked in December 2004 when celebrity chef Jamie Oliver got into hot water for his TV advert promoting Sainsbury's smoked salmon. The farm on Loch Hourn, Inverness-shire, that featured in the advert, it emerged, was being investigated by the Scottish Environmental Protection Agency for polluting local waters. Meanwhile, Oliver himself eschewed farmed salmon in his London restaurant.) While supermarket fish counters are awash with farmed salmon, some local wild populations teeter on the brink of extinction. 'A salmon's life seems to be a very short and a very hard one', reflected an American angler in the 1930s. 'He lives, on the average, about eight years; and from the time he is spawned in the river there seems to be something or someone continually at him.'[11] Chapter Three (Unfortunate Salmon, or the salmon's dangerous world) looks at the human activities that have complicated the life of 'this unfortunate fish' (as Charles Dickens dubbed it).[12] Nonetheless, the return of the wild salmon has also grabbed the headlines, recent reappearances in once-blighted European rivers hailed as a welcome antidote to the usual tales of ecological woe.

Native Americans who have harvested salmon from the Columbia in the Pacific Northwest for millennia had a metaphor for their river. It was a 'great table' at which various bands came to eat at different times. In every salmon river, a range of groups have jostled for position at the great table, often elbowing others aside in their bid to secure the lion's share of the fare, leaving those pushed away with the crumbs from the feast. Chapter Four (Disputed Salmon, or who owns the salmon?) examines these tensions and altercations (and, in the process, looks at various methods of capture). For excluded Britons, zealously guarded fishing privileges epitomized the elite's arrogant appropriation of fundamental human rights. In North America, social conflict has been supplemented by racial strife between aboriginal and Euro-American fishers.

Often aligned against both subsistence and commercial interests were those who fished with a rod and line for pleasure (the subject of Chapter Five, Sporting Salmon, or the fish that hooked us). No angler would dissent from Walton's view that the salmon has been 'accounted the King of freshwater fish'.[13] In fact, the sporting fraternity is largely responsible for consolidating its lofty reputation. Since the early nineteenth century, fly fishing for salmon has been the preferred pastime of an assortment of royalty, politicians, aristocrats, industrialists, novelists and poets. Many aficionados have recorded the joys of fishing for this gamest of game fishes and dipping into this literature helps explain its lure.

Finally, fish culture means a lot more than artificial propagation. Chapter Six (Cultural Salmon, or a fish swims through us) ponders the range of meanings we have attached to the salmon and how we have represented it through various cultural media – from first salmon ceremonies to the poems of Ted Hughes. The notions of 'salmon nation' and 'people of the salmon' – conveying how profoundly the fish has sustained cultures in mind as well as body – is usually synonymous with North America's Pacific Northwest. Yet the beliefs and cultural forms of the indigenous peoples of northern Japan and the Siberian Far East were just as enmeshed with salmon. And in northwest Europe, cultural expressions provide glimpses of former salmon nations. This biography of a species that has acquired multiple identities explores the salmon's evolutionary, ecological and human stories. Ranging from Nova Scotia to Norway, from Korea to California, and from prehistory to the future, it compiles a multifaceted portrait: a veritable 'compleat salmon'.

1 Biological Salmon

'Of all the families of fishes', insisted David Starr Jordan, the leading nineteenth-century American ichthyologist, 'the one most interesting from almost every point of view' was Salmonidae (Salmonid).[1] His British counterparts agreed. Salmonidae's members, remarked Francis Day, a former Inspector-General of Fisheries in India, 'are universally admitted to rank second to none in value, whether regarded as food, as affording sport, or interesting objects for study'.[2] From the angler's standpoint, Salmonidae are the most interesting of all fish families because more game fishes belong to it than to any other – its ranks include trout, grayling and char as well as salmon.[3] Particularly intriguing from the biologist's viewpoint is that a number of family members (genera) are anadromous (Greek for 'running upward'). Like the alewife, striped bass, sturgeon and shad, salmon are conceived and born in freshwater but spend most of their adult lives in the ocean, eventually returning to rivers to spawn. As such, they get the best of both worlds. 'Like some persons of honour and riches', observed Izaak Walton, 'which have both their winter and summer houses'.[4] This arrangement reflects the family's residence within a belt spanning the northern hemisphere, where oceans are generally more productive than freshwater habitat (the reverse applies to southern latitudes). On the Atlantic side, Salmonidae's

The oldest-known salmon fossils:
1. Juvenile specimen of *Eosalmo drift-woodensis* from Driftwood Canyon, British Columbia.

historic range lies between the Arctic and 40 degrees, dropping to the 30th parallel in the Pacific.

Salmonidae's fossil record is scanty. The oldest known specimen (just 15 cm long) dates back 50 million years. The bones of *Eosalmo driftwoodensis* were found in the Eocene sediments of British Columbia's Driftwood Creek canyon in the 1930s, but a paleoichthyologist (Mark Wilson) first identified it in 1970

2. Adult specimen of *Eosalmo drift-woodensis* from a site in southern British Columbia.

(formally naming it in 1977). This particular salmonid, which lived in the lakes of western Canada, resembled today's grayling and belonged to the class of bony, ray-finned fishes known as teolosts, which also include perch, pike and catfish. The discovery of the fossils of juvenile as well as adult fish suggests that, at this stage, Salmonidae were probably non-migratory.[5] Fossilized skulls from an epoch between 5 and 24 million years ago – when Europe, Greenland and North America were connected – indicate that Salmonidae's various genera were already established. The 12-million-year-old sabre-toothed salmon (*Smilodonichthys rastrosus*), a leviathan ten feet long and weighing 180 kilograms (the first fossils were found in Oregon in the 1960s), may be a direct ancestor of two of today's Pacific species, the sockeye and chinook.

The north Pacific and the north Atlantic house discrete species of salmon, the two genera to which they belong corresponding, in turn, to the respective oceans: *Salmo* and

'Salmo a Salmon' and 'Salmulus' (a Smelt), from Francis Willughby, *De Historia Piscium Libri Quatuor*, edited by John Ray (1686).

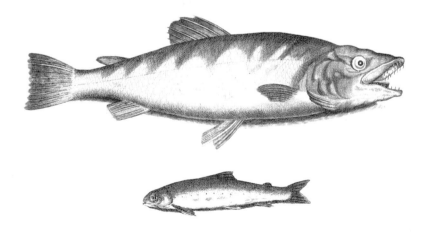

Oncorhynchus. Of the five species comprising the Atlantic's *Salmo*, only one is a salmon (*Salmo salar*); the rest are trout. The southernmost limit of the historic range of *Salmo salar* on the North American side is probably Massachusetts. On the European side, *Salmo salar* frequents the North Sea, Baltic Sea, Barents Sea and White Sea and roams as far south as the rivers of northern Spain that empty into the Bay of Biscay. Despite its distribution from the Gulf of Finland to the Gulf of St Lawrence, North American and European stocks of *Salmo salar* lack the differences that would divide them into sub-species.

Pliny the Elder bestowed the Atlantic salmon's formal name in the first century – perhaps inspired by reports from Julius Caesar's legions, which, marching through Gaul in 56 BC, had noticed the riveting spectacle of a new variety of fish leaping up the Garonne (in Aquitaine, Pliny noted, salmon was the preferred fish).[6] *Salmo* (indicating the genus) probably has its origins in *Salmona*, the name of a river in east-central Germany ('Salm' in German) that is a tributary of the Moselle (a usage that appears in Ausonius of Bordeaux's fourth-century poem, 'Mosella'). *Salar* (denoting the species) may derive from *salire* ('to leap').[7]

Ten species belong to *Oncorhynchus*, which ranges from southern Korea to southern California. Seven are salmon, the remainder are trout.[8] *Oncorhynchus*, derived from two latinized Greek words: 'hooked' and 'snout', was coined in 1861 by George Suckley, a former assistant surgeon and naturalist with the US government's Pacific Railroad Survey that explored the vast territory between Minnesota and Puget Sound (1853–6). Because the only Pacific salmon he observed were spawning males, whose most striking feature is a hooked lower jaw (kype), Suckley failed to appreciate that male (cock) and female (hen) salmon are sexually dimorphic (physical characteristics vary at different stages of their life cycle) and relegated females and immature males to a different species. Notwithstanding Suckley's basic error, *Oncorhynchus* stuck.

The scientific nomenclature for the seven Pacific species is an adaptation of the common names applied by the Koryak peoples of the Kamchatka peninsula in eastern Siberia. These names first appeared in Europe, translated phonetically into German, in Georg Wilhelm Steller's account (1743/4), posthumously published, of Kamchatka's natural and human history.[9] Johann Julius Walbaum, a physician-naturalist from Schleswig-Holstein, first recorded them as official scientific names when he observed the various species in the Kamchatka River (1792).

Oncorhynchus tschawytscha (pronounced cha-vee-cha) is variously known on the North American Pacific coast as King, Spring, Sacramento, Quinnat and Tyee, but most commonly as chinook (after the dominant tribe of the Columbia River basin). Historically, it was distributed from Point Hope in the Alaskan Arctic to southern California's Ventura River. On the other side of the Pacific, its range extends from the Japanese island of Hokkaido northward into the Bering Sea and round Siberia's

The chinook salmon (*Oncorhynchus tschawytscha*).

westernmost tip into the Arctic Ocean. Chinooks are now also found in the southern Pacific, having been transplanted to New Zealand's South Island in the early 1900s and, later, to Chilean waters for aquaculture (escapees have started to colonize rivers descending from the Andes).

The largest salmon by far, the chinook can weigh as much as 45 kilograms. (The heaviest catch on record is 57 kilograms.) Its spawning runs are the earliest of the Pacific species, beginning in spring, and among the longest. Before being stymied by dams in the 1930s and 1940s, chinooks migrated 1,600 kilometres up the Columbia, and still travel between 2,400 and 3,200 kilometres up the (dam-less) Yukon. *Oncorhynchus nerka*, though sometimes known as red due to the colour of its flesh (especially in the canning industry), is most often referred to as sockeye (the anglicization of the Chinook word *Sukkegh*). Sockeye are more abundant today than chinook – though much smaller at between two and five kilograms – and the species most highly prized by aboriginal and commercial fishers alike. After chum (see below), *Nerka* travels the greatest distances upriver and spans the Pacific from Kamchatka to British Columbia.

Oncorhynchus gorbuscha is commonly known as pink. Spawning males develop a pronounced hump between head and

The sockeye salmon (*Oncorhynchus nerka*).

The pink salmon (*Oncorhynchus gorbuscha*).

dorsal fin – hence the other vernacular name of humpback (*gorbuscha* in Russian). The smallest of the Pacific species at one to five kilograms – and the most abundant – it follows a very regular, two-year spawning cycle, attaining sexual maturity earliest and venturing least far upstream. Transplanted to the Barents Sea and Newfoundland in the late 1950s, a few specimens have been logged in British waters. *Oncorhynchus kisutsh* (also known as coho, medium red and silver) spawns latest, in autumn, often in smallish streams with short runs, and does not venture far into the sea during its six-year life. After the chinook – the species to which it is the most closely related though considerably smaller at 3 to 6 kilos – the coho is the least plentiful. Cherished especially

The coho salmon (*O. kisutsh*).

The chum salmon (*Oncorhynchus keta*).

by anglers, the acrobatic coho was released in the Great Lakes in the 1960s to revive moribund sport fisheries.

Chum and dog are the most popular North American vernacular names for *Oncorhynchus keta* (*keta* means 'the fish' in the language of the Nanai peoples who inhabit the Amur River region where China and the Russian Federation meet). Chum probably stems from the Chinook word for striped – *tzum/sum* – inspired by the flamboyant streaks and blotches that decorate the fish's body in spawning mode. Dog, the preferred Native Alaskan term, refers partly to its big head but mainly denotes the enlargement of the teeth during spawning, especially those at the tip of the lower jaw, which, Steller observed, assume canine fang shape and may measure half an inch. (That Native Alaskans routinely feed their sled dogs chum salmon adds extra currency.) The chum and its closest relative, the pink, are the most broadly distributed of the Pacific species, extending as far south on the American side as Monterey Bay, California, yet also frequenting the Arctic Ocean from Siberia's Lena River to Canada's Mackenzie. On the Asian side, chum even frequent the southernmost islands of Japan. Like the pink, it spends very little time in freshwater, heading seaward when just an inch long. This gives chums and pinks more time to feed and grow in the sea, explaining why they are the most numerous of Pacific salmon (they also undertake the longest migrations).

A further two species are found only in the Asian Pacific: *Oncorhynchus masou* and *Oncorhynchus rhodurus*. *Oncorhynchus masou*, known as the masu or ocean-running yamame (the latter a Japanese-Kanji name meaning 'mountain woman fish') is an anadromous fish similar to the coho. In Japan, masu (*sakura masu*) is popularly known as the cherry salmon because the appearance of spawning adults coincides with cherry blossom season.[10] The masu (whose leitmotif is bold transversal stripes) is the most southerly of the Pacific salmon in distribution, with a large run on North Korea's Tumen River and a presence in Taiwan's Tachia River. *O. rhodorus* comes in two forms, the lake-living biwamasu (var. *rhodorus*) and the stream-dwelling amago (var. *macrostomus*), whose vermilion spots set it apart from the more widely distributed yamame. Yet identifying the various Pacific species and distinguishing them from their Atlantic counterpart often requires close examination of gum colour as well and the number of teeth and anal fin rays. Most readily grasped, though, is the difference in shape between the salmon

Ocean-run *Salmo salar*, from *A History of the Fishes of the British Isles*, 4 vols (1860–65), by Jonathan Couch, a physician from the Cornish fishing village of Polperro. His skill in the dissection and depiction of fish won him a fellowship of the Linnaean Society.

of the two oceans: *Salmo salar* is sleeker – more hydrodynamic.

THE SALMON'S LIFE CYCLE

Other, more important differences stem from their life cycles. Whereas Pacific salmon without exception die after spawning, up to 6 per cent of their Atlantic relatives survive and return to the sea. Another feature setting them apart is the portion of their lives spent at sea. The Atlantic salmon typically resides in fresh water for two to three years before going to sea. In northern Norway and Labrador, it can remain there for eight years – much longer than any Pacific salmon species. Atlantic salmon also spend more time in freshwater on their return to their spawning

Atlantic salmon life cycle.

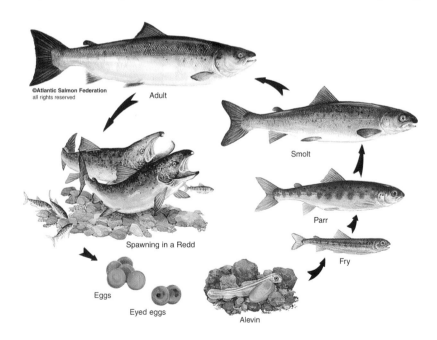

©Atlantic Salmon Federation
all rights reserved

Adult

Smolt

Parr

Spawning in a Redd

Fry

Eggs

Eyed eggs

Alevin

22

grounds. The time spent in fresh and saltwater is partly determined by the relative availability of food in these two mediums.

After migrating downstream as young fish, salmon roam the oceans for between one and six years, often travelling thousands of miles. They mingle with others besides fish from their home river. Fish from both sides of the Atlantic share a common feeding ground off western Greenland. Pacific species also become jumbled up. Then, as they mature sexually, salmon perform an astonishing feat of biological reorganization, separating into distinct groups of compatriots that head for their respective home streams (examples of straying to the other side of the Atlantic are extremely rare). Salmon re-enter their rivers year round, but some only run in late summer or autumn.

A profound physiological transformation during a sojourn in brackish water equips the salmon for re-entry into freshwater. Because the salt concentrates in their bodies are usually higher than in the surrounding freshwater, they do not need to drink while in rivers. Water flows into their tissues toward these salt concentrations. In the ocean, however, the salt concentration in the water is much greater than in a fish's body, so the water flow is reversed. To rectify this water loss, the marine salmon must reverse the operation of its salt pumps to absorb water, expelling excess salt through its gills.

Many Atlantic salmon face relatively short upstream journeys compared to their Pacific cousins. European salmon rivers are often less than a hundred miles long, allowing for a fairly leisurely pace. On Scotland's Dee and Spey, daily rates of between 0.18 and 0.74 kilometres have been logged. By contrast, some Pacific populations face staggering journeys. Averaging between 16 and 32 kilometres daily, they may clock up a much higher rate if their spawning grounds lie far upstream. At Dawson City, 2,415 kilometres up the Yukon,

King salmon jump the flume of a mining company on Copper Creek, Alaska, c. 1907.

64.
KING SALMON
ATTEMPTING TO JUMP
THE FLUME OF KENAI
MINING AND MILLING CO.
COPPER CREEK, ALASKA
COPYRIGHT 1907
BY LILLIE N. GORDON

chum were registered travelling a 80-kilometre daily average in the 1890s. Salmon also need tremendous energy reserves because of the potential delays they face in the shape of floods, low water and obstructions; they may wait weeks below a waterfall until conditions are right for an ascent. Laboratory experiments in which a sockeye swam at a rate of 2.9 kilometres an hour against a stiff current for nearly 13 days without pause (equivalent to 1062 kilometres) suggest the fish's amazing strength. Another experiment involved observing sockeye on a fish-way's treadmill; they climbed continuously for five days – the equivalent of 6,648 metres. Eluding predators and surmounting obstacles also demands bursts of speed. And salmon can make faster and more abrupt turns than any other fish.

On leaving the sea, salmon stop eating. A century ago, many fish biologists and anglers found it barely credible that a fish could go for so long – sometimes up to a year – without eating. 'It would be inexplicable, indeed', remarked the American sportsman Charles Hallock, 'if salmon alone of all creatures, were not required by nature to fortify and strengthen themselves for the supremest act of physical existence'.[11] Thomas

Huxley, the British scientific all-rounder, was less impressed by their ability to cope on an empty stomach, pointing out (1860) that they had gorged at sea while swimming 'in a species of animal soup'.[12] Peter Duncan Malloch, a self-taught Scottish authority, conducted some unusual early twentieth-century experiments to confirm the fasting theory. He dropped prawns and sweets off a bridge over the Tay, commenting that 'they were readily taken, but after a few nibbles the fish allowed them to fall to the bottom'.[13] As the salmon lives off the fat stored in its tissues during its ocean pasturage, its stomach shrinks to the size of a finger to make room for the eggs or milt and gonads that eventually occupy most of the body cavity. At the point of spawning, the ovaries may constitute over 15 per cent of the hen's live body weight, while the cock's testes are five times heavier than when he quit the sea.

On reaching the coast, salmon run the gauntlet of a predatory horde. If they survive seals, otters, porpoises and herons, they face human fishermen armed with nets, traps, spears and rods. In addition to dams and weirs, other impediments may confront them. Construction of the Canadian Northern Pacific Railroad triggered a massive rockslide that plugged Hell's Gate canyon, 240 kilometres up British Columbia's Fraser River, effectively preventing further upstream migration of the major portion of the sockeye's autumn run in 1913. This was the world's greatest salmon run and spawning sockeye backed up for 16 kilometres below the blockage, choking the river with red bodies 'packed together like seeds in a pomegranate' (to quote a Canadian poet).[14]

A blocked Hell's Gate presented too daunting a challenge. Nonetheless, as Walton remarked, salmon can surmount obstacles 'even to a height beyond common belief'.[15] For many (like Pliny) this became the fish's defining activity (many pubs

Leaping Alaska salmon.

along British salmon rivers are called 'The Leaping Salmon'). Andrew Young of Invershin, Scotland, manager of the Duke of Sutherland's nineteenth-century salmon fisheries, reckoned that an upward, slanting leap of 12 feet (3.6 metres) was within the capacity of most salmon, though few succeeded at the first attempt. Their indefatigability was legendary. In the 1920s, a British salmon biologist observed repeated efforts to scale a six-foot fall that lasted an hour.[16]

This uncanny ability was once regarded as proof of supernatural powers. Another fanciful and surprisingly tenacious view was that the salmon held its tail in its mouth and bent itself taut like a bow before jerking itself upward by suddenly letting go. In his early seventeenth-century English epic poem,

Poly-olbion, Michael Drayton described this accomplishment at the falls ('Salmons leape') that rear up as fish enter the Tivy in west Wales.

> Heere, when the labouring fish doth at the foote arrive,
> And finds that by his strength he does but vainly strive;
> His taile takes in his teeth; and, bending like a bowe
> That's to the compasse drawn, aloft himself doth throwe,
> Then springing at his height, as doth a little wand
> That bended end to end, and started from man's hand,
> Far off itself doth cast; so does the Salmon vault:
> And if, at first, he faile, his second Summersaut
> Hee instantlie assaies; and, from his nimble Ring
> Still yarking, never leaves untill himselfe he fling
> Above the streame full top of the surrounded heape[17]

Others believed that airborne salmon propelled themselves higher by flapping their tails. In actuality, responding to sound vibrations, they negotiate falls by jumping from the spot where most water is falling, diving deep to reach the upward moving water that provides a vital added boost. So, a waterfall considerably lower than 3.6 metres may offer an insuperable challenge if the launch pool is too shallow.

The leaping salmon is undergoing a metamorphosis in appearance and physiology (particularly pronounced in the male) that is often described as a monstrous deformity. The fins thicken and the skin becomes spongy, mucous-covered and leather-like in texture, virtually absorbing the scales. Breeding teeth replace feeding teeth, which, especially in the male, are considerably larger and sharper. The head lengthens into a snout and the body becomes more compressed, developing a cartilaginous hump. Most mature males develop extended

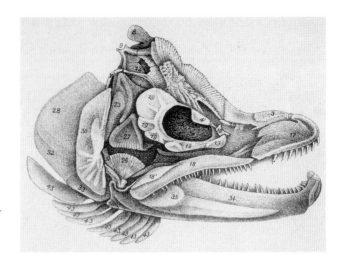

Skull of male Atlantic salmon, from Francis Day, *British and Irish Salmonidae* (1887). Day was a retired Indian Army surgeon and former inspector-general of fisheries in India. He drew the skulls himself.

'Salmo salar (*Der Hakenlachs*)' from *Ökonomische Naturgeschichte der Fische Deutschlands*, vol. 3 (1785), by M. E. Bloch, a Berlin physician who supplied an accurate descriptive and visual account of all German species. The use of silver and gold accentuates the sheen of the salmon's scales.

upper and lower jaws. The apex of the lower jaw's dentary bone enlarges and curves upward to form the grotesque-looking kype that so impressed Suckley (Walton compared it to a hawk's beak).[18] Meanwhile, the upper jaw's premaxillary bone grows and dips downward to accommodate the kype with an interlocking socket, though the mouth no longer closes properly.[19]

Dazzling transmogrifications in hue accompany this bodily reconfiguration. The silver-sided oceanic fish assumes a striking range of darker colours. Pinks turn slate grey on their backs and sides and creamy white on the ventral surface. Chum undergo the most stunning make-over. Within days of entering freshwater, their sides display jagged red and black (sometimes green and purple) bars, with patches of dappled grey and yellow (hence the archaic name, calico salmon). Chinook and coho assume the trademark dark red that lends spawning rivers a blood-streaked appearance. Sockeye go bright red and their heads olive green. Atlantic salmon also change colour, though the female generally becomes darker and duller than the male. So profound were these changes, remarked Steller, that unless one

A cock salmon in spawning livery.

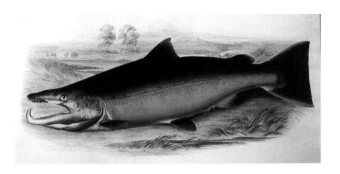

was familiar with their life cycle 'they would never be taken for the same fish that enter the rivers'.[20]

Sir William Jardine (1800–1874), seventh Baronet of Applegarth (Dumfriesshire, Scotland), drew an exquisite picture of a male weighing 7.25 kilograms taken from a pool in the River Annan, one December during the 1830s. Captured at the height of its spawning phase, the fish sported a brilliant scarlet and orange hue on his sides while his upper parts were brownish. Jardine, who later served as president (1860) of the Royal Commission of Inquiry into the English and Welsh salmon fisheries, supplied a vivid accompanying written description of this ephemeral coat of many colours: 'The colouring, when newly taken from the river, was beautiful beyond description, and is not to be conveyed by any representation: independent of the brighter tints and rich purplish-grey running along the lateral line, the whole body was, as it were, glazed over with a delicate crimson-pink, changing and fading with the life of the fish'.[21]

Changes in colour may well be connected to the switch to freshwater, a respiratory response to lower oxygen content. Since salt water contains more oxygen, salmon in the sea go through 40 breathing cycles per minute. In freshwater, they must compen-

'Duelling males'. The first sketch represents a salmon charging a rival; the second, a male covered with honourable scars, after the wars are over. From Lewis Lloyd, *Scandinavian Adventures* (1854).

THE CHARGE.

AFTER THE BATTLE.

sate for their reduced rate of respiration and red pigments such as cartenoid are effective carriers of oxygen. Shedding oceanic colours also provides superior camouflage.[22] Charles Darwin took a different line, though, contending that the male's colours (and hump) were co-called secondary sexual characteristics, i.e. male attributes that females find attractive or that males think females will find attractive. He emphasized the extreme pugnacity of cock salmon, citing reports of a day-long struggle between two males and rivers littered with the bodies of dead combatants. Darwin also interpreted the kype as a defensive weapon against the 'fangs' of sexual competitors.[23]

According to some salmon biologists, 'preliminary' pairing begins at the spawning grounds.[24] Others reckon that they team up much earlier, possibly on entering freshwater. Nobody has suggested, though, that salmon are monogamous. But they are very fussy about where they mate. Spawning grounds must supply exactly the right kind of water and gravel (meaning pebbles rather than small fragments of stone). The water must be clear, cool and fast flowing – sediment and vegetal growth associated with sluggish water inhibit hatching – and devoid of predators. Riffles (a patch of shallow but fast-moving water) are ideal for digging a redd (a Celtic term for spawning pit now in universal use). If the water is deep enough, the hen assesses the gravel's

'Female Salmon Cutting a Redd with her Tail', from P. D. Malloch, *Life-History and Habits of the Salmon, Sea-Trout, Trout, and Other Fresh-water Fish* (1912).

quality by assuming a vertical position and fanning her tail furiously to dislodge it. She then plunges down to 'feel' with her anal fin; gravel must be sufficiently loose to allow circulating water to oxygenate the eggs yet not so loose that digging a trough would be like trying to excavate a hole in dry sand.

If satisfied with the gravel's condition – and having identified a satisfactory mate – the hen 'cuts' a redd. Lying on her side, sometimes in water so shallow there is barely water to cover her back, she fans her tail to create upward suction. Assisted by the current, this action dislodges gravel and creates gaps, also serving to loosen and lift off any silt and sand that may jeopardize the survival of eggs and fry (ova suffocate without sufficient oxygen). Redds can be circular or trench and furrow-like, and are between 8 and 30 centimetres deep. According to some commentators, female salmon can shift gravel as large as a half brick. This sounds implausible. But heavy objects are much lighter in water and the current is a great help. Having deposited gravel the size of eggs in a trough of water, C. F. Walsh of Dundee recorded that 'holding a dead fish by the head and on its side, I gently undulated it, and I found the stones were puffed away as if by a gentle breeze of wind'.[25] She sometimes interrupts her cutting to drive off female intruders.

Wedded to conventional notions of the division of labour between male and female, many Victorian scientists insisted that the cock fish dug the redd. However, Walsh, who witnessed hundreds of nineteenth-century spawnings, reported that 'I never saw the male fish take any part in the work; the *fanning* up of the gravel is all done by the female. I say *fanning*, because I never saw any *boring* of the head into the ground'.[26] Dissenters from Victorian scientific orthodoxy believed that the spawning male's head injuries were sustained fighting off rivals rather than from digging. Walsh's views are no longer disputed.

Meanwhile, like a rutting stag, her mate stands guard to repel other males. These contests could be bloody and exhausting. One Victorian observer recorded that 'there was one fellow who appeared to be king. Whenever [another male] attempted to come too near the female he made a rush at him, seized him and shook him as a retriever would shake a hare'.[27] Other contemporaries disputed the gravity of these encounters, claiming that the kype's function was precisely to prevent males from inflicting grievous harm, because it prevented them opening their mouths wide enough to grab their opponents with their savage teeth.

When done digging, still lying on her side, the hen sinks to the bottom of the trough. By flexing her tail, she extrudes thousands of eggs (900 for each 450 grams of body weight is the norm). The male then squirts a milky substance called milt (sperm) over them. Other Victorian accounts relate a more intimate act. The male moves alongside and vibrates his body vig-

A spawning pair of Atlantic salmon lie on their sides, virtually out of the water, the female's excavating tail the only submerged body part; from Malloch's *Life-History and Habits of the Salmon . . .* (1912).

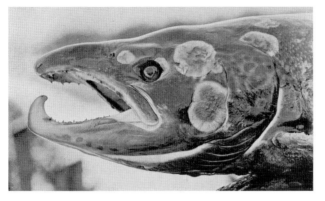

orously against her for a few seconds (a muscular spasm preparing for milt delivery that has been described as 'quivers just like the final shudder of a dog after it has been in the water').[28] Rubbing against each other, they eject ova and milt simultaneously in an act sometimes referred to as an orgasm (though a British angler living in Scandinavia, Alexander Keiller, was keen to reassure that 'nothing that could be construed as sexual intercourse took place between them').[29] Another male may release his cloud of milt at the same time and dominant males may mate with other hens if there's a surplus. The female fills in the redd with what remains of her battered tail.

The grim reality that spawning colours, however resplendent, cannot disguise, is that salmon bodies are steadily disintegrating. Worms infest the gills. Flesh becomes soft, watery and white from loss of oil. The fungus, *Saprolegnia ferox*, appears on the flanks and head – the external manifestation of the microbe *Bacillus salmonis pestis* (so-called salmon disease). This microbe enters a skin abrasion and spreads, attacking the tissue. Having established itself on dead tissue, the fungus invades living tissue and continues to spread after death.

'Head of a Male Grilse (7 lb.) Afflicted by Fungus, December 1905', from Malloch's *Life-History and Habits of the Salmon* . . . (1912).

Two scraped sections reveal the thickness of the encrusted fungus, much of which developed after the fish had died; from Malloch's *Life-History and Habits of the Salmon* . . . (1912).

Dead bodies of spawned pink salmon washed up in the shallows of the Cheakamus River, British Columbia, 1963.

Having lost between a third and a half of its body weight, the spawned out salmon is emaciated and exhausted (digging a redd can take three days and nights). If a member of a Pacific species, it invariably dies within weeks – literally starving to death. Roderick Haig-Brown, an American angler, described the death of a female chinook ('Spring') in her spawning pool, standing guard over her eggs (though sitting like a bird on thousands of eggs is not an option).

> The strong current caught Spring as she went down from the surface. It drew her to itself, rolled her over and swept her on and she no longer resisted. Her tail moved once or twice, feebly, but all the urgencies, all the desires that had driven life thru her were spent. So she lay quietly across the stream flow, drifting as no strong salmon does and the

water opened her gill plates and forced under them and she died.[30]

These mass die-offs were not a pretty sight. 'The passage of the river is a sickly spectacle', remarked Hallock, 'maimed and decaying fish in myriads offending sight and smell, and befouling the entire length of the water course from the sea to its springheads.'[31]

Walton's reference to the spawning bed as a 'grave'[32] initially seems odd but is actually highly appropriate for a place of birth in view of this symbiotic relationship between death and new life. Once the ova hatches, the salmon's life cycle goes through seven stages: alevin, fry, parr, smolt, grilse, mature adult and kelt. The time it takes to run its course varies from just over a year to a maximum of ten. The duration of each stage also varies enormously. The offspring of the spawning season of 1913 on the Wye returned to breed in phases over the next six years – a staggering mechanism to militate against fluctuating extremes of bumper and lean crops of young fish.

A salmon's age and life history can be determined by scrutinizing the rings on its scales under a microscope (a variation on counting tree rings, though salmon produce several each year). As fish grow, the number of scales remains the same but each one gets bigger. The proximity of the rings – which resemble roughly circular concentric ridges – reveals a good deal. Periods of rapid summer growth are marked by pronounced, widely spaced rings. Colder periods with less abundant food are marked by fainter, more closely spaced rings, a wide band and a narrow band indicating a typical year.

The first three stages of the salmon's life are exclusive to freshwater habitat. The pink, pea-sized eggs remain buried a few months, depending on season and water temperature. For suc-

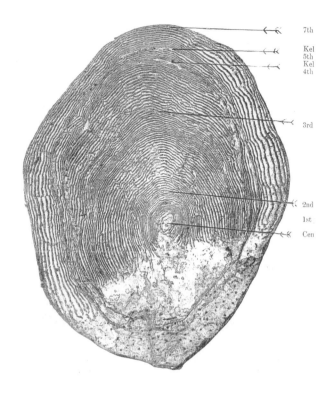

Scale rings, from J. A. Hutton, *Salmon Scales as Indicative of the Life History of the Fish* (1909). Hutton, the son of a Manchester cotton merchant, devoted his life to the study of salmon, amassing an unparalleled knowledge of Wye populations.

7th

Kel
5th
Kel
4th

3rd

2nd
1st
Cen

cessful spawning, the water must be under 58°F. The creature that hatches, the alevin, is effectively an orphan, a large-headed and bulging-eyed infant that must sustain itself on the orange yolk in its umbilical sac during its first few months. The alevin then becomes a fry. Measuring about an inch and a quarter at first, its basic food is diatoms – tiny brown algae (phytoplankton) that thrive in the bright light of open-canopied stream banks.

When a fry is as long as a man's middle finger – usually by the end of its first summer – it changes into a parr. The parr (or samlet) begins the journey downstream, floating tail-first so

Atlantic salmon eggs.

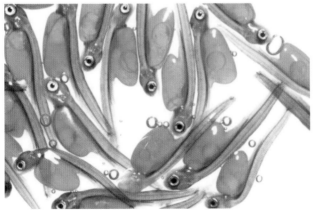

Pacific salmon alevins.

'Young Salmon, About a Week Old', from Frank Buckland, *Manual of Salmon and Trout Hatching* (1864).

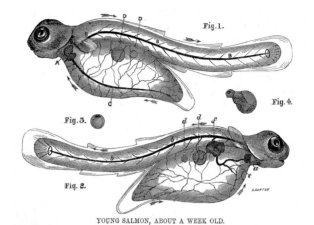

YOUNG SALMON, ABOUT A WEEK OLD.

Salmon fry.

that water does not enter its gills. Though readily identifiable from the bluish-olive fingerprint-like marks that run down its sides (another reason for the alternative name, fingerling), young parr are easily confused with other juvenile Salmonidae. Sir Humphry Davy, the English chemist renowned as the inventor of the miner's safety lamp, argued that the parr was the hybrid offspring (mule) of salmon and trout.[33] But the first artificial raising of salmon eggs (1836–7) confirmed that parr were young salmon.

Feeding on freshly hatched flies, the parr measures four to ten inches by the time it reaches estuarine waters. Here, a profound and relatively rare kind of internal change converts it into a fish that can live in saltwater. Smolt also assume the livery (to use Victorian parlance) of the adult salmon, which is better suited to life in the sea. A blue back, white belly and silver sides provide perfect camouflage (the silvery, iridescent scales result from an increase in the amount of guanine – a whitish substance).

The grilse is an adolescent male that attains sexual maturity early and makes a precocious attempt to spawn after just a few months at sea (or a single winter). Like the parr, the grilse perplexed fish biologists for centuries, though no one still insists that they constitute a separate species. The grilse's tail is more forked than a mature adult salmon's and its wrist is thinner, lending it 'a dainty and delicate appearance, quite different from the somewhat rotund outline of the sea-trout, and more graceful than the decidedly athletic proportions of the adult salmon'.[34] The grilse probably quits the ocean so soon as part of an evolutionary insurance policy. The production of a reserve supply of willing and able males ensures that any potentially unfertilized eggs are not wasted.

A spawned salmon is called a kelt, or, sometimes, in the case of the male Atlantic, a kipper ('black, cadaverous fish with

'Parr or Samlet', from Sarah (Mrs T. Edward) Bowdich, *The Fresh-Water Fishes of Great Britain* (1828). Bowdich accepted the orthodox view that the parr ('skegger') was a distinct species rather than a young salmon.

heads seemingly enormous, and lank, slimy bodies, repulsive to themselves and abhorred by the anglers').[35] Spawned salmon lose control over their swim bladders and float belly up. They bounce against rocks and flap in the shallows. Those few kelt that survive (exclusively *Salmo salar*) begin to repair themselves as they head downstream, completing their restoration at sea. This includes shedding the kype, as it would be impossible to breathe and feed in the ocean if still encumbered with it. At this 'well-mended' stage, the characteristic silvery hue has returned, making them practically indistinguishable from 'clean' fish. Under 10 per cent of mended kelts return to spawn again. And very few are male. This seems odd, initially, for females appear to have expended far more energy digging and refilling redds. But fighting off competitor males is evidently more tiring.

The salmon's life in freshwater is far better understood than its oceanic existence. It has become increasingly clear, though, that they don't loiter in coastal waters. The recapture of tagged fish raised in hatcheries in Canada's Maritime Provinces in the early 1900s indicated that Atlantic salmon travelled up to a thousand miles from their natal streams.[36]

The longest recorded distance is 5,630 kilometres: a chinook tagged in the central Aleutian islands was recaptured a year later in Idaho's Salmon River. Salmon tend to congregate in areas of up-welling, where prevailing offshore winds drive surface waters away from land, allowing currents to rise vertically to the surface, bringing up nutrients from the bottom. The urge to migrate is evidently connected to the urge to mate, which presumably becomes more powerful than the desire to feed.

The rate of return, though, is extremely low. Salmon eggs are remarkably tough. To test their resilience, one researcher dropped an egg from waist height, recording that 'it rebounds quite in the manner of a tennis-ball, and externally remains equally undamaged'.[37] But their survival rate is nonetheless poor. Some are washed downstream and others are never fertilized.

'Severn Salmon', from Sarah Bowdich's *Fresh-Water Fishes . . .* (1828). Bowdich was convinced that the true colours of a fish could only be captured at the moment that it was removed from the water. Her plates are hand-coloured and use gold and silver foil to recreate the metallic shine and shimmer of fish scales.

Many creatures prey on them, including their parents. The tiniest alevin and the largest parr are vulnerable to trout and pike as well, also eagles, eels and otters. The fierce otter that Tom encounters in Charles Kingsley's fantasy novel, *The Water-Babies* (1863), explains that salmon are

> great fish, nice fish to eat. They are the lords of the fish, and we are the lords of the salmon . . . We hunt them up and down the pools, and drive them up into a corner . . . and we catch them, but we disdain to eat them all; we just bite out their soft throats and suck their sweet juice . . . and then throw them away, and go catch another.[38]

Young salmon that elude river-based predators and make it to the ocean are eaten by fish ranging from Greenland shark to cod. Figures for the sockeye indicate that, of approximately 3,600 eggs laid, 106 smolt enter the sea, of which 10 will return to their natal stream. Of these, eight will die during the upstream journey, leaving two to spawn – the minimum number required to sustain existing populations.

Hector Boethius (Boece), a Scottish ecclesiastic, provided the first more or less reliable account of this 'strange' fish's 'procreation and nature' (1527).[39] Boethius – doubtless familiar with salmon from the rivers Dee and Don, which empty into the North Sea at Aberdeen, where he served as the university's first principal – explained that 'salmond' 'with maist fervent desire and appetite returnis to the samyn placis, quhair thay wer generit'.[40] In the fourth volume of his magisterial *Historiae Animalium* (1558) – a compendium of all existing classical and medieval knowledge of a zoological nature, upgraded with contemporary observations – Conrad Gesner (1516–65), a polymath scholar from Zurich, supported Boethius' account of freshwater spawning. And Walton cited what may have been the first tagging experiments to support the belief that 'every salmon usually returns to the same river in which it was bred'. Ribbon, he reported, was tied to the tails of juveniles caught in weirs as they swam seaward; about six months later, some were recaptured with ribbons intact at the same spot.[41] By the nineteenth century, ribbons had been replaced with copper and brass wire that often inflicted serious cuts. Other researchers simply sliced off the small, fleshy fin in front of the tail (adipose fin).

The *parent* stream and the *natal* stream are usually but not necessarily the same. And if fertilized eggs are relocated, the salmon that hatch will return to the stream where they were born rather than to the stream where they were conceived. In 1880, Jordan referred to this 'extraordinary instinct' to spawn where they were born as 'one of the most difficult problems in animal psychology'.[42] Most nineteenth and early twentieth-century ichthyologists scorned the notion of a homing instinct, reasoning that fish did not possess large enough brains to navigate so precisely. Scientific orthodoxy held that salmon did not venture far out to sea, and had the choice of any number of rivers for spawning.[43] Given, though, that they remained within the orbit of their natal stream, by default some would return there. As well as seeming impossible, there appeared to be no good motive for a return to the natal stream.

These scientists lacked an understanding of local adaptation and its ecological and evolutionary importance. For them, chinook that spawned in California were no different from chinook that spawned in Alaska. This failure to appreciate differences was not entirely unreasonable. After all, different species and populations intermingle in the ocean to an enormous degree. Spawning rivers are also shared: all five species in the North American Pacific use different parts of the same river or the same parts at different times. Believing that it made no odds if fertilized ova from Alaskan chinooks were deposited in a stream in California, the first artificial propagation programmes in the late nineteenth century assembled a melting pot of stock. This weakened the gene pool (there are no known cases of hybrids between species or within species in the wild).

Having finally embraced natal stream theory, it remained for ichthyologists to explain its mechanisms. Salmon lack the cerebrum and neo-cortex organs that permit higher intelligence. But they have excellent eyesight, even in turbid water, and can see colours. More significantly, their sense of smell is acute. Our ocularcentric modern western culture underestimates the power of smell. Yet smell is the biotic world's oldest sense, perfected hundreds of millions of years ago by fish that developed the first noses. All but the most primitive fish forms have two external nostrils connected to a nose brain, one on each side of the head, and can smell in 'stereo'.[44] 'Smell', remarked

Jean Jacques Rousseau, 'is the sense of memory and desire', and one of the first to identify this as the vital tool was Frank Buckland, Victorian natural scientist extraordinaire. Using the expression 'to follow his nose', Buckland provided a charming, if erroneous image of a salmon glued to an odour trail like a hunting dog. 'Thus a salmon coming up from the sea into the Bristol Channel would get a smell of water meeting him. "I am a Wye salmon", he would say to himself. "This is not the Wye water; it's the wrong tap, it's the Usk. I must go a few miles further on", and he gets up steam again.'[45]

Though this line of inquiry was not pursued at the time, it was resumed in the 1950s, when Arthur Hasler confirmed the integral role of olfactory imprinting. The internationally renowned freshwater ecologist had his brainwave while walking along a mountain stream near his hometown in Utah. Stimulated by the scent of native wildflowers, he started thinking about the power of smell to evoke childhood memories. Freshwater minnows could be trained to distinguish between water from two rivers. But when their olfactory organs were damaged or destroyed, they proved unable to find their way home. On the other hand, blinded fish with smell organs intact returned successfully. Further experiments exposed hatchery-raised coho to odorant chemicals before release into Lake Michigan. Two years later, when they were ready to return to their native streams, Hasler's team laced one stream near the original release site with morpholine and another with phenethyl alcohol. Of the returning fish that were monitored, over 90 per cent were found in the stream carrying the chemical to which they had been exposed as hatchlings.[46] Hasler's findings indicated that each stream has a unique chemical fingerprint derived from its peculiar mix of soil, flora and fauna, whose presence is unaffected by pollution and fluctuating water levels. During their return journey, salmon follow the sequence of smells in reverse order, progressively getting closer to the only right smell.

The odour hypothesis seems much more believable with regard to a salmon that spawns at no great distance up a big river than in the case of a salmon that faces an upstream journey of 1,600 kilometres, followed by an additional trip up a small tributary. How can the home stream's signature smell remain discernible in an estuary into which a major river pours the waters of an enormous catchment area? Eel larvae manage to find their way back from the Sargasso Sea to their freshwater habitat in Europe across 8,000 kilometres of ocean. And they can detect unbelievably low concentrations of alcohol (comparable to one shot of vodka in Lake Erie – the world's eleventh largest lake). So the salmon's ability to discriminate between smells should not be underestimated. Hasler drew a homely analogy: 'The first fragrance of the morning coffee is tantalizingly sharp, but as it permeates the air, one ceases to be aware of it: the olfactory organs have become fatigued to it. However, other scents – bacon and eggs, oatmeal, pancakes – can cut through the coffee odour and be perceived immediately despite the fatiguing or accommodation of the olfactory sense to the coffee.'[47] Like the eel's, the salmon's sense of smell is so keen that it can detect the most dilute concentration of home stream odour amongst a myriad of other smells.

How, though, do salmon find their way from open sea to coast? And how do they know which direction to follow on reaching the shore? Can we accept that the odour trail begins thousands of kilometres out at sea? In 1960s experiments, gill nets with descending horizontal sections mostly captured salmon in their upper layers, suggesting that they navigate using a sun compass mechanism. Hasler's experiments with white bass in a lake indicated that fish – identified with yellow floats – that

Salmo (salm) and
Sälmling (Samlet),
from Conrad
Gesner, *Tomus IV:
Et Ultimus oder
Fisch-Buch* (1670).

were observed on cloudy days or that had opaque plastic eye caps attached had trouble orientating themselves. 'That an animal is actually able innately to accomplish something for which men require instruments, charts, and tables', remarked Hasler, 'is quite incredible.'[48] That salmon (like migrating birds and turtles) employ celestial navigation methods is the most popular current explanation of their movement from ocean to coast. Then the distinctive odour of the home stream takes charge.

The evolutionary purpose of homing is tied to the fact that each river has its distinctive salmon 'stock' or 'population' ('races' and 'tribes' were the terms employed when this notion was first mooted in the 1920s). A population is a unit comprising the individual members of a species living in a specific locale that share a genetic ancestry and are much more likely to breed amongst themselves than with individuals from another comparable unit. There is only one species of Atlantic salmon, but those that spawn on the North American coast and their European counterparts are genetically different. The timing of spawning runs and smolt migrations are simple ways to identify different populations.

Physical and behavioural traits carefully honed over generations confer a survival advantage on a specific stream's population. Yet home-stream fidelity also has its downside. When a river is lost to a log jam or dam, its stock is also lost. By the same token, salmon can fail to exploit fresh opportunities. Experiments in eastern Canada (1938–9) indicated that spawning salmon only used one of a river's two branches. Though the second branch was available at that time, a barrier had effectively excluded all salmon from it until the late 1920s. So, even though this tributary's potential spawning grounds had been open for a decade, salmon ignored them in deference to their time-honoured destination. In this sense, the umbilical link between population and stream can be self-destructive. To write off a perfectly suitable spawning river forever, however, makes no evolutionary sense. And so each salmon population generally includes a few enterprising individuals capable of colonizing new habitat.[49] This explains why a small number (about 2 per cent) occasionally 'stray' elsewhere to spawn. This also permits eventual recolonization of a stream whose local population has been extinguished. Straying also facilitates the occupation of salmon habitat that humans create. Before the mid-nineteenth century, the Ballisodare River in County Mayo, Ireland, had never seen a salmon. Where it empties into the Atlantic, a series of natural falls and rapids rule out upward migration. By 1855, though, thanks to installation of fish passes, hatchery raised salmon could enter what has become one of Ireland's most productive salmon rivers (while ova planted higher up could descend).

We tend to think of evolution as a process that takes thousands of years and transpires without human agency. Yet it can occur within a single human lifetime. Within 30 generations, distinctive life-history traits have evolved among specific ocean running populations of chinooks transplanted to New Zealand between 1901 and 1907. They also look different. Females undertaking the longer spawning runs tend to be bigger and to lose more body weight during their migrations. That neither physiological identity nor range are frozen in time will become clearer when this discussion of the wild fish is supplemented (and complicated) in the next two chapters by coverage of salmon raised in hatcheries and produced on fish farms. The meat and drink of the next chapter, though, is the salmon in its most familiar role. This initial examination of the biological salmon has only incidentally been concerned with food – dwelling mostly on why salmon *don't* eat after they re-enter freshwater. Now the edible salmon swims into view as we explore its identity as sustenance for other creatures.

2 Edible Salmon

The relationship that most Europeans have with salmon today is with the steaks and fillets they buy from the supermarket fish counter. Cod remains Britain's top seller in terms of volume. Yet salmon is hot on its heels with nearly a third of fresh fish sales. What sets the current era of salmon abundance and high consumption apart from any previous period of plenty, though, is the salmon's provenance. Virtually all salmon sold in Europe nowadays is farmed. Between 1980 and 1999, as aquaculture burgeoned, salmon consumption within the European Union increased nearly ten-fold (trends mirrored in North America). This is not the first time, however, that a fish with a prestigious reputation (not least as a culinary delicacy) has been readily available. Consumption had previously boomed on a global scale in the late nineteenth century. As Ernest Dunbar Clark remarked:

> The can of salmon is to be found from African jungle to Andean plateau, from Madagascar to Manhattan. It graces impartially the sumptuous banquet of the rich and the humble repast of the peasant. To both it brings the rich flavor of the sea and the healthful elements found therein. They go with the explorer over the trackless tundra and ice, or through the barren desert of the

Mongolian steppe, frozen or subjected to day after day of intense heat the fish within remains fresh and palatable, tempting and satisfying when opened'.[1]

In 1911, the Alaska Packers Association of San Francisco, the biggest salmon canning company of its day, cited an 'eminent scientific authority' on the benefits of tinned salmon: 'Within the entire range of preserved food it would be difficult to name an article of greater dietary value and cheaper than Salmon, with the exception of milk'.[2] Yet the eating of salmon in a form modified from its original living self by those who may never have seen a live salmon predates the advent of canning. Eaters of salmon – whether tinned, farmed or wild – are now far more widely distributed that the fish itself. But intake of salmon is as old as humankind.

Our use for salmon has not been confined to its flesh, however. We have also worn its skin. In the native villages of the Russian Far East and northern Japan, curing salmon skins and making clothes from their leather is a dying art, practised by a few elderly grandmothers. In western Europe, though, this craft is being rediscovered. The last word in modish beachwear may strike us as outlandish – the salmon skin leather bikini – but falls squarely within a long tradition of garments fashioned from the fish.

ANIMAL CONSUMERS

We may be the only creature that dons the fish's skin, but we are not the only one that eats its flesh. The huge Alaskan brown bear standing belly deep in a fast-flowing stream, scooping salmon out with its paws or snatching them in its jaws, is an arresting image in countless natural history documentaries.

A brown bear snatches a salmon from an Alaskan river.

The most famous setting for this primordial encounter is the McNeil River Falls on the Alaska Peninsula, where up to a hundred (normally solitary) bears congregate in July and August, jostling for position to gorge on migrating chums as they try to ascend. (Canadian poet Tim Bowling evokes the image of a 'fur-swaddled landlord of Imperial Russia raising a half-eaten sockeye like a goblet of wine'.)[3] So extravagant is this moving feast that these brown bears attain 680 kilograms in weight, making them the world's largest carnivorous mammals. Bruins are peerless consumers. A female brown bear – smaller than its male counterpart – can eat 34 kilograms a day. In fact, salmon comprise 90 per cent of a bear's food prior to hibernation and the quantity of available salmon determines the number of cubs born the following spring.[4]

The bear is just the biggest and most charismatic of an array of animals that benefit from the salmon's bounty. One of the world's greatest wildlife spectacles is the late autumn gathering of some 3,000 bald eagles in the trees that line the Chilkat River near Haines in southeast Alaska, where they gorge themselves on the cluttered hordes of spawned-out chum. The pieces of flesh that the eagles discard are pounced on by a range of mammalian scavengers. Over 130 species include salmon in their diets – including salmon themselves. Spawned-out carcasses sustain the next generation of salmon by fertilizing the water and promoting algal growth. The scat of the birds and mammals that feed on salmon, in turn, supplies valuable micronutrients for the soil. Salmon help make the land by transferring carbon and nitrogen – life's basic elements – from a biologically rich oceanic environment to more impoverished inland ecosystems: hence the title of Richard Manning's book: *The Forest That Fish Built* (1996). Salmon are literally part of many other species, permeating the economy of nature.

ABORIGINAL CONSUMERS

Human subsistence economies have been just as firmly grounded on salmon. This is because tremendous quantities crowd together at predictable times in readily identifiable and relatively accessible places at a stage in the spawning run when the flesh is still in top condition. The first evidence of human consumption from Europe, dating back to 16,000–9,000 BC, is a fragment of harpoon bearing a salmon motif from a cave in northern Spain. The earliest known evidence from the North Pacific is nearly as ancient. At the village of Ushki, Kamchatka, Russian archaeologists have unearthed hooks and other tools made from salmon bones and vertebrae, as well as bone fragments over 11,000 years old. In 1960, archaeologists digging at the Milliken site in the Fraser River Canyon found the charred midden remains of 9,000-year-old cherry stones. These had presumably been tossed into the fires over which the coastal

Salish, who fished there seasonally, were roasting the sockeye whose runs (August and September) coincided with the ripening of the wild cherry crop (and cherry pits survive better than salmon bones). More recently, archaeologists working on the Alaska Peninsula have unearthed some 300 village sites whose artefacts indicate that the economic and cultural lifeblood of these Aleut communities has been salmon for 6,000 years.[5]

Written accounts by European explorers and early visitors evoke a picture of North American salmon cornucopia. Frontier folklore describes a 'pavement' phenomenon; rivers teemed so thick with salmon that it was almost possible to walk across without wetting your feet. Others evoked the analogy of a puddle squirming with tadpoles.[6] In the late nineteenth century, a member of the United States Fish Commission evoked a real scenario of original plenitude almost as impressive in describing the dog (chum) salmon in a southwest Alaskan stream before commercial exploitation began:

> As we advanced [upstream] they increased in numbers until it seemed as though in places one could no longer advance through them. It was simply full of dog salmon in all stages, from those in but a short time from the sea to the spent and dying. . .We followed the stream about two miles and it seemed in places as though we were wading in salmon; they would often strike one's leg with considerable force, swim between one's feet, and in walking we at times stepped on them, and frequently touched them with the foot.[7]

Pacific coast Indians characterized salmon as 'lightning following one another'. Yet it would be ahistorical to say that Native Americans the length of the west coast have always enjoyed a

A Hupa tribesman watching for ascending salmon in northern California, c. 1923.

special relationship with the fish. Beyond coastal Alaska, salmon-dependent economies evolved gradually, the proportion of salmon bones among the faunal remains at midden and hearth sites investigated by archaeozoologists in British Columbia steadily increasing relative to those of other fish and to land mammals between 10,000 and 3,000 years ago. Fully-fledged salmon economies may have appeared even later in southern Oregon and northern California. The emergence of salmon nations followed the development of techniques for preserving an often abundant but only briefly available and usable food supply for year-round consumption.[8]

Salmon became equally indispensable to the indigenous Ainu of southern Sakhalin, the Kurile Islands, Hokkaido and Honshu, who finally capitulated to Japanese control in 1789. In the winter and spring of 1725–6, some 200 Ainu died of starvation in Ishikari province (Hokkaido) following a lean autumn run.[9] The Ainu word for salmon, *chipe*, comes from *shi-e-pe*, meaning 'the main food that we eat'.[10] A picture in Ezo Fuzoku's *Juni-ka-getsu* (*Twelve Months of Ainu Manners and Customs*, *c.* 1872) shows an Ainu fisherman spearing salmon from the bank at night with a spear called a marek by the light of a torch made of rolled birch bark; the marek had a special pivoting hook that stopped the fish wriggling off. These rivers were so dense with salmon during the late nineteenth century that a British explorer, echoing the US fish commissioner in Alaska, recorded the disconcerting sensation, while wading across the Shikarubets River, of having them rub against his legs or pass between them. He appreciated the skill of Ainu fishermen operating from dugout canoes with spears, but felt that there were so many fish it was 'easier to catch than to miss'.[11]

To ensure a supply during the long, hard winters, the Ainu hung some of their catch from trees to freeze, carving off pieces to thaw and grill as required. They also suspended salmon to air-dry or smoke from the rafters of their huts (compounding their dwellings' unsavoury 'scent' to the British explorer's nose).[12] They savoured the roe too, eaten boiled and salted and mixed with potatoes. Over in coastal Oregon, indigenous peoples produced a type of cheese from salmon eggs. Not every part of the fish went into their mouths, though.

The Irish poet W. B. Yeats believed that the humble fisherman, though without worldly goods, was still free to dream of 'shoes made from the skin of a fish, or a coat made from the glittering garment of the salmon'.[13] Yet such items were the stuff of daily life for many northern coastal communities, no more exotic than Yeats's fisherman's lowly brown shawl that seemed too prosaic for poetry. The wearable salmon complemented the edible salmon in aboriginal and other traditional cultures. In the absence of readily available livestock hide and textile fabrics, Icelanders and inhabitants of Quebec's Gaspé peninsula made clothes and footwear out of fish skin. So did the Ainu, who relied on the thicker and tougher skin of spawned salmon (*hotchare*) for making winter boots (*chepkeri*).

A westerner particularly impressed by salmon skin attire was Henry Lansdell, a nineteenth-century British missionary and traveller whose destinations included the Siberian far east. The primary purpose of Lansdell's visit was to inspect the region's notorious prisons and forced labour camps and his ground-breaking account was the key to the instant success of the tale of his eastward journey beyond the Urals to the Pacific. But there was more to *Through Siberia* (1882) than salt mines and wretched exiles. Lansdell packed in a wealth of ethnographic observations. He characterized the salmon-dependent Gilyak peoples of the lower Amur regions as 'perfect heathens' who were 'dirty beyond description'. Yet forming the book's frontispiece is a picture of the author resplendent in a birch bark (lampshade-shaped) summer hat and sporting the salmon skin 'costume of the Gilyaks' that he bought at Tyr.[14]

London's Victoria and Albert Museum recently restored and displayed a nineteenth-century salmon skin coat from the Gilyak

The 19th-century British explorer and missionary Henry Lansdell posing in a salmon skin costume of the Gilyak people of eastern Siberia, from his book *Through Siberia* (1882).

peoples of the lower Amur basin (near Vladivostok). This fancy coat – perhaps a female marriage robe – was fashioned from 60 large skins (it has not been possible to identify the species). The most elaborately decorated part – the upper back – consists of pieces of glued-down skin shaped like fish scales. Though the garment – probably tanned with brains or fish eggs – had been in storage since 1905, textile conservation curator Marion Kite characterized as 'strong and still supple enough to allow the coat to be handled for examination'.[15] Nor did clothing exhaust the non-edible uses of salmon. Indigenous cultures across the northern

Pacific used salmon skin for waterproof covers to protect cargo transported by boat and sled. The Ulchi of Siberia's Amur River region – whom the ancient Chinese derided as 'fish skin Tartars' – also made boat sails from salmon skin and extracted glue (*darpu*) from the bladder.

EURO-AMERICANS DISCOVER SALMON

North America's Euro-American explorers wore clothing and footwear made of fabric and conventional leather but they too subsisted on salmon. The first Euro-American to comment on the

First American drawing of a Pacific salmon, in a page from the journals (16 March 1806) of the Lewis and Clark expedition. William Clark's drawing of a 'white' salmon (a.k.a. silver salmon, salmon trout and coho) (*Onchorhynchus kisutch*).

palatability of Pacific salmon was Captain William Clark. In May 1804, he left St Louis, Missouri with Captain Meriwether Lewis to explore the massive chunk of uncharted territory recently acquired from France. Fifteen months later, the expedition crossed the Continental Divide, heartily sick of the dwindling supplies of salt pork, flour and cornmeal, on which they fell back in the absence of freshly killed game. As a guest at a Shoshone encampment on the Lemhi River (in present-day Idaho), Lewis was given a 'small morsel of the flesh of an antelope boiled and a piece of a fresh salmon roasted'. This modest repast, 480 kilometres from the ocean, tasted delicious to a man who had eaten nothing of late but dried berries. (The meal was also pregnant with larger meaning for it 'perfectly convinced me that we were on the waters of the Pacific'.)

There would be plenty more salmon on the expedition's menu as they got closer to the Pacific – though mostly dried. At first, this liberal supply of protein was a godsend. But the Corps of Discovery soon tired of its monotonous diet, on which Lewis blamed their incorrigible dysentery. Still, they had little choice. Large game animals were scarce and fresh fish unavailable because the salmon were in their post-spawning phase and rapidly decaying and dying. Most fresh salmon they encountered were anything but delectable, so Lewis and Clark declined many that Indians tried to sell them (they suspected they were washed up). They preferred to buy dog meat and were ecstatic when they shot gulls and ducks.

As the party descended the Snake River and then joined the Columbia, the signs of an all-encompassing salmon culture and economy enveloped them. Scaffolds laden with drying salmon lined the river. Curing operations were particularly thick around Celilo Falls, where the arid climate was conducive to curing split fish in the open air without salt. Piles of dried salmon pounded

Under the salmon row. Frank H. Nowell depicts a group of Eskimo children lined up under a rack of drying salmon in Alaska, c. 1906.

Drying salmon in Alaska, early 20th century. A sizeable drying operation run by Euro-Americans shows all stages of the process.

into thin shreds between two stones also dotted the landscape. Sheets of this fish pemmican were layered in rush baskets lined with stretched salmon skin, a waterproof substance. Twelve tightly packed baskets with a total weight of 41–45 kilograms

Indian dip-netting at Celilo Falls, Columbia River, Oregon, *c.* 1899. Fishermen perched at the end of wooden scaffolds that protrude far out over the churning water underlines dip-netting's precarious nature.

formed a stack. Preserved in this manner, pemmican remained 'Sound and sweet Several years'.[16] Pemmican, as well as being traded with whites at the mouth of the Columbia, was big in inter-tribal commerce. Tribes from far and wide came to Celilo Falls to trade for it. From western Montana and the Dakotas arrived horses, buffalo meat and buffalo hides. Meanwhile, obsidian, slaves and shells were brought up from the south coast, while blankets and beads came down from the north.

The dip net was the Indian's fishing gear of choice at cascades, where up to 3,000 fishermen would cluster. At Celilo Falls, to gain access with their nine-metre-long dip net poles to the fish they couldn't see in the swirling river, local Indians built wooden scaffolds and platforms mounted on poles that extended out above the roaring waters. When he felt the weight of an invisible fish, the fisherman would yank out his net. To land a 27-kilogram salmon – even when secured to the scaffolding with ropes – was no mean feat. And fatalities were not uncommon. To white observers, though, the living was easy compared with that of Indians who eked out an existence further inland by hunting deer or grubbing up roots ('indeed', commented the novelist Washington Irving, 'whenever an Indian of the upper country is too lazy to hunt yet is fond of good living, he repairs to the Falls to live in abundance without labour').[17]

MEDIEVAL AND EARLY MODERN EUROPEAN FISHERIES

Over in Europe, salmon maintained a powerful presence into historic times. As in North America, both natives and incursive peoples subsisted on the fish in northern Britain. 'We cannot be quite sure that Caesar ever dined off salmon', remarked Alexander Russel, editor of *The Scotsman* and a member of the Edinburgh Angling Club, in the 1860s. 'But', he added, 'we are warranted to please ourselves with conjuring up the image of the Roman soldiers, as they kept watch and ward by the wall of Hadrian and of Antoninus, ever consoling themselves with a

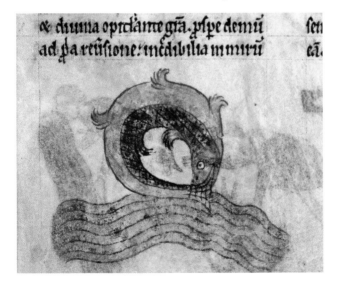

An Irish salmon, bent like a bow in readiness for flinging itself upriver, from Gerald of Wales's *Topographia Hibernica* (c. 1196–1223).

65

cut from the tail of a twenty pounder cooked in a three-legged camp kettle.'[18] Subsequent invaders took careful note of salmon assets. The Domesday Book (1086) listed the new Norman kingdom of Britain's salmon fisheries in its natural resource inventories. A century later, Gerald of Wales registered the salmon-rich rivers of Ireland.[19]

Salmon loomed particularly large in the worldly desires of religious men. Prior to dissolution, monasteries owned many of the weirs, fishing boats and fishing rights on British and Irish rivers. Cong Abbey in Ireland, a twelfth-century Augustinian monastery, with a peak population of 3,000 monks, maintained a fish house (still standing) with a trap across the River Cong's main current. When a fish was caught, a cord triggered a bell in the kitchen. In his *Life of Thomas à Kempis* (1680), Francisco Tolensi reported that many canons sang the psalms with such joy and devotion it was as if they were eating salmon. Thomas, the German author of the early fifteenth-century *Imitation of Christ* (after the Bible, perhaps the most influential of Christian texts) supposedly replied, 'Thank God, these psalms are like salmon to me' (he lived on the north Rhine and the play on words works best in German, where the word for psalm is *Salm*).[20] This love of salmon was doubtless encouraged by the Church's proscription of the consumption of meat from terrestrial animals not just on Fridays but during Lent and major feast days, which added up to about a third of the year. Eating fish as a substitute had been authorized in the seventh century, creating a regular demand that pond-raised carp could not satisfy.

Though the Romans shipped salted salmon home from Gaul, long-distance trade really picked up in the medieval era.[21] Between the early and late middle ages, consumption patterns shifted from fresh local (often freshwater) fish to preserved fish from more distant, usually maritime sources. Scotland was a leading exporter. International commerce in dried salted cod is far better known, but fifteenth-century Glasgow merchants despatched salted salmon to Flanders, France and Holland. Salmon rubbed with salt and pepper were smoked (kippered) with peat and shipped in a wooden barrel (kitt). Leathery and very salty, this preserved form bore little resemblance to today's soft, mildly smoked strips.

Pickled salmon eventually replaced salted and kippered.[22] Scottish fish were boiled in salt and packed with a topping of brown vinegar; sometimes, spices were added. As late as 1712, Aberdeen's fish merchants exported 1,270 barrels (with a capacity of 113 kilograms each) to Bilbao, Marseilles and Venice. In his authoritative early eighteenth-century account of British social and economic conditions, Daniel Defoe noted that domestic trade also flourished between Perth and 'all the towns where they have no salmon'.[23] Other northeastern ports of Britain shared in this wealth. Before the industrial revolution, Newcastle was famous for salmon rather than coal and the 'Newcastle Way' denoted a method of pickling boiled salmon with allspice, black pepper and vinegar. Perth and Berwick-on-Tweed shipped the fresh article to London aboard sailing ships. With a stiff north wind, the journey from Perth in the 1760s could take just 60 hours.[24] If the prevailing winds were wrong, though, the catch was unloaded, boiled, pickled and kitted and sent off again when the winds were favourable. In the 1780s, Perth merchants shipped the first salmon packed in ice to London's Billingsgate fish market.

Numbers sufficed for prodigious local consumption too. In the rivers of Caithness and Sutherland in northern Scotland, Defoe found salmon 'in such plenty as is scarce credible, and so cheap, that to those who have any substance to buy with, it is not worth their while to catch it themselves'.[25] An oft-cited measure of the salmon's ubiquity is regulations restricting the amount that could be fed to servants. In mid seventeenth-century Stirling, noted a captain in Cromwell's army during the English Civil War, 'Burgomasters (as in many other parts of Scotland) are compell'd to reinforce an ancient Statute, that commands all Masters and others, not to force or compel any Servant, or an Apprentice, to feed upon Salmon [from the River Forth] more than thrice a Week'.[26] In *The Tale of Old Mortality* (1816), a historical novel set in 1679, Sir Walter Scott confirmed that the fish, being so plentiful, was 'generally applied to feed the servants, who are said sometimes to have stipulated that they should not be required to eat a food so luscious and surfeiting in its quality over five times a-week'.[27]

In fact, these particular salmon were far from luscious. Employers usually fed working folk readily captured kelts that they bought up in vast quantities for a song. Tough as old boots, they tasted terrible – and, in the case of kippered kelts, dreadfully salty too. As such, they were considered unfit for consumption by the respectable classes ('no wonder . . . apprentices objected to eating this stuff more than twice a week', commented the Devon-based angler, Kenneth Dawson, in the 1920s).[28] Unless we appreciate the miserable quality of the servants' salmon, the salmon's reputation as the most delectable of fish is hard to square with their wholesale revulsion.[29]

THE CANNED SALMON

The long-suffering pre-industrial servants and apprentices who could barely stomach the thought of yet another salmon meal were not, however, the biggest British consumers of modern times. That distinction belongs to the late nineteenth-century industrial working class. Not only did they eat their salmon with a good deal more relish than their predecessors. Their salmon was also very different. It came out of a can and had lived in the Pacific. Lewis and Clark – who were particularly disgruntled at having to eat spoiled salmon pemmican for their Christmas dinner in 1805 – did not envisage that salmon could become a lucrative commercial commodity. But American entrepreneurs following in their wake saw a terrific business opportunity in the teeming silver masses.

Canning's origins lie in Napoleon's difficulties feeding his far-flung armies and navies. Hard-tack, smoked fish and salted meat kept spoiling, so he offered 1,200 francs to whoever could devise a fail-proof method of food preservation. Nicholas Appert won in 1809 by sealing and boiling food in glass jars. But glass jars often broke and were heavy to ship. By 1815, Appert was preserving food in the lighter and more durable tinplate canister (eventually abbreviated to can). But Americans pioneered in the canning of seafood, initially cod, oysters and lobster on the east coast. The Hume brothers – whose Scottish ancestors had caught salmon on the Tweed and Tay – established the west coast's first salmon cannery on California's Sacramento River in 1864. When Robert Hume was growing up in Maine in the 1850s, salmon were so rare there due to overfishing, dams and pollution from sawmills that he'd never eaten one. Yet northern California's salmon runs were already drying up rapidly too; gold mining polluted their waters and rapacious hydraulic methods obliterated spawning grounds. Within two years, the Humes shifted operations to the mouth of the Columbia, where they and others converged to 'get a whack at this new El Dorado, all seeking a fortune to be made from the capture of the scaly beauties'.[30]

Rudyard Kipling provided a striking account of this region's definitive commercial enterprise during his North American tour of 1889. Returning to Portland, the Columbia River steamer on which he rode halted at a fish wheel to pick up the previous night's catch. During a 20-minute stopover to unload the cargo at a cannery downriver, Kipling ventured inside to observe. Notwithstanding the 'slippery, blood-stained, scale-spangled, oily floors, and the offal-smeared Chinamen', he marvelled at the speed and efficiency of the operations.

> When our consignment arrived, the rough wooden boxes broke of themselves as they were dumped down under a jet of water, and the salmon burst out in a stream of quicksilver. A Chinaman jerked up a twenty-pounder, beheaded and de-tailed it with two swift strokes of a knife, flicked out its internal arrangements with a third, and cast it into a blood-dyed tank. The headless fish leaped from under his hands as though they were facing a rapid.[31]

Yet prior to mechanization of this operation in 1903 with the invention of the 'Iron Chink', tremendous quantities were

Chinese men working at machinery with cans of salmon in background, probably in Washington or Oregon. *c.* 1913.

chucked back into the Columbia because the size of the catch exceeded cannery capacity (though protests complained of the smell, not the profligacy). This windfall attracted huge congregations of bears. So did the offal that canneries dumped into the river, only to see it wash up on the incoming tide.

The first overseas customers for the distinctively red cans were in Australia, New Zealand and South America (to prevent rusting in the early days, cans were lacquered with a mixture of turpentine, linseed oil and red lead, indelibly associating tinned salmon – and its labels – with the colour of the fish's flesh). At first, Richard Hume recalled, the more distant British 'did not take kindly to the American product'. But thanks to the vision and perseverance of one particular firm, Pelling & Stanley of Liverpool (Hume's British agents), Britons soon emerged as the top buyers of canned Pacific salmon. Pelling & Stanley was the forerunner of John West Foods, Britain's leading canned salmon retailer. John West was a Scot who settled in Oregon, where his business ventures in the 1860s included a cannery. West won a gold medal for his salmon at the Oregon State Fair in 1874 and Pelling & Stanley bought the rights to this premier brand on his death in 1888.[32]

Pelling & Stanley's genius, Hume explained, was to recognize the potential of a new product that offered a highly nutritious food (protein equal to that of beef steak and lamb chops) at between a half and a third of the price of fresh salmon. Nevertheless, it took Pelling ages to shift his first 500 cases (a case contained 48 450-gram tins) – possibly because salmon had become so scarce in Britain that few urban workers would ever have tasted it. Each day, Pelling walked around his enormous pile to see if it had shrunk a little. Slowly but surely, ordinary Britons cultivated a taste for a fish that, in its local incarnation, had acquired a luxurious image. As fewer and fewer

John West's award-winning 'Oregon Brand' tinned salmon.

salmon were running up the Mersey from the Atlantic, more and more were entering the river in cans from the Pacific. By the mid-1870s, Britons were eating 450,000 cases a year.[33] Tinned salmon was a signature food of the British empire as well. Cases were unloaded on the wharves of Calcutta, Cape Town and Melbourne as well as Liverpool. Kipling hailed the mighty Columbia as 'the river that brings the salmon that goes into the tin that is emptied into the dish when the extra house guest arrives in India'.[34]

Sticking labels on cases of canned salmon, Columbia River Packing Association, Astoria, Oregon, 1941.

Stacks of canned salmon, Columbia River Packing Association, Astoria, Oregon, 1941.

This growing availability might appear to signal the democratization of the salmon as a foodstuff. But the distinction between tinned and fresh was firmly maintained. In the British general election of December 1923, fought principally over the incumbent Conservative Party's plans for tariff reform as a

EAT MORE SALMON

"WE CAN'T! WE CAN'T! The Conservatives are going to put a tax on it and make it cost us more"

But the tax is not on yet. And if you vote **"LIBERAL"** in this election it will never be put on.

The tax on Tinned Salmon is one of the new proposals of the Conservative Party. It is a very mean proposal. They say nothing about **fresh** Salmon, which can only be bought by well-to-do people. It is **Tinned** Salmon that is to be taxed and made more costly. This is too bad! A tin of Salmon is so convenient. When your husband's mother turns up unexpectedly, and there is nothing cooked in the house, you only have to send Doris for a tin of Salmon and the rest is easy. And very nice, too!

The Conservatives want to make that tin of Salmon more costly. It doesn't matter to them. They can buy fresh fish and anything else that they fancy. But **your convenient little tin is to be taxed.**

And they are going to put a tax on other things, too. They are going to tax **TINNED APRICOTS,** and **RAW APPLES,** and **CURRANTS** and **RAISINS,** and many other things.

THIS silly game must be stopped. The only people who can stop it are the ...

LIBERALS

The LIBERALS will not tax any of these things.

IF YOU WANT CHEAP FOOD
VOTE LIBERAL

The salmon as a party political pawn. A British Liberal Party leaflet produced for the 1923 General Election campaign exploits tinned salmon's image as the people's food.

solution for unemployment, tinned salmon – the people's food – featured in Liberal Party campaign materials. 'Eat More Salmon', the brochure admonished. Yet the voice of the people replied 'We Can't! We Can't! The Conservatives are going to put a tax on it and make it cost us more'. The proposed tariff, the Liberals explained, applied only to tinned salmon, fresh salmon being the food of 'well-to-do people'. The caption then under-

Hoisting salmon onto a ship at the wharf, Petersburg, Alaska, early 20th century.

CANNED SALMON
Our greatest food from the sea

CANNED SALMON
Our greatest food from the sea

lined tinned salmon's integral place in the average Briton's diet. 'A tin of salmon is so convenient. When your husband's mother turns up unexpectedly, and there is nothing cooked in the house, you only have to send Doris for a tin of salmon and the rest is easy. And very nice too!'

Tinned salmon retained its populist credentials in Britain vis-à-vis fresh and smoked salmon from domestic waters. For some sophisticates, it was a sign of provincialism and lowly status. 'Cider and tinned salmon is the staple diet of the agricultural classes', ridiculed the managing editor of a London newspaper (*The Daily Beast*) in a satirical novel set in the 1930s.[35] For others, it was a badge of pride. 'I've never denied my origin and background', remarked Harold Wilson, Labour prime minister between 1968 and 1976. Born into a lower-middle-class family (and the first prime minister to attend a state school), Wilson announced to the *Observer* newspaper (11 November 1962) that 'I don't do much socialising and my tastes are simple. If I had the choice between smoked salmon and tinned salmon, I'd have it tinned.'

Though Wilson did not reveal his favourite type of salmon, Red salmon (sockeye) and Medium Red (coho) dominated the late nineteenth and early twentieth-century cannery catch so thoroughly that salmon became synonymous with deep red and marketing less intensely coloured species became more difficult

The firm plump flesh of a noble salmon,
cooked to such tenderness that it melts in your
mouth. "*You were right when you said
we'd have something tasty tonight.*"
Sealed in its own rich natural oils —
that's the goodness of John West's
Middle-cut. "*Anyone would think that
they never saw food before.*" A juicy
red slice of salmon is a full-sized meal for a
hungry man. "*Well, I feel fine after that!*"

Insist on the best, and buy

JOHN WEST'S
Middle-cut SALMON

A John West
tinned salmon
advertisement,
1938.

once preferred supplies began to wane (connoisseurs, though, treasure the rare, white fleshed Ivory King). Chum, with its pale pink, less firm flesh and the lowest fat content of any salmon species (imparting a milder flavour), traditionally occupied the lowest commercial grade.

THE CULINARY SALMON

The versatile salmon lends itself to numerous culinary interpretations. 'Doris' in the 1920s may simply have emptied the contents of her can onto a plate and served the meat as chunks on a bed of lettuce (though Harold Wilson garnished his with vinegar). But a bizarre early nineteenth-century method of cooking fresh salmon required even less effort. One of the 'wonders' that the Fraser family of Lovat showed off to their guests was a 'voluntarily cooked Salmon' at the falls of Kilmorac on the Beauly River, Inverness-shire:

> For this purpose, a kettle was placed upon the flat rock on the south side of the fall, close by the edge of the water, and kept full and boiling. There is a considerable extent of the rock where tents were erected, and the whole was under a canopy of overshadowing trees. There the company was said to have waited until a Salmon fell into the kettle and was boiled in their presence.[36]

Illustration from a recipe for salmon loaves, from the Alaska Packers Association's book, *Canned Salmon Recipes* (San Francisco, 1911).

Nonetheless, most consumers of fresh salmon have been required to put in a little more work. In the eighteenth and nineteenth centuries the preferred method on the Tweed was simplicity itself. Just landed salmon were plunged into a cauldron of salted water boiled over an open fire. (This 'kettle of fish' was sometimes the centrepiece of a river bank picnic or fête champêtre, particularly popular with monks from Melrose Abbey: Walter Scott's novel *St Ronan's Well* (1824) describes one of these jolly occasions.) Scalding seals the exterior by coagulating the albumen, a jelly-like substance sandwiched between the flakes of flesh, thereby ensuring that its goodness is preserved in the form of a creamy curd rather than being dissolved into the water. The fish was then served in the brine in which it was cooked. 'This', announced Thomas Stoddart, 'is salmon in perfection.'[37] Scott agreed, prepared to countenance, at the very most, a dash of lemon juice or vinegar. Others preferred to eat their salmon a couple of days after it had been caught, once the curd had dissolved into the oil, enriching the flesh.[38]

New ways of serving salmon continue to emerge. Mark Kurlansky fears that, as cod stocks dwindle, fish and chips will lose its meaning and place within Britain's national cultural pantheon because the fish in the dish is synonymous with cod.[39] But cultural traditions are flexible. Late eighteenth-century recipes for that typical dish of English Jewry, fried fish, recommended salmon as well as cod and mackerel.[40] Salmon has not yet been tossed into the fish and chip shop's hallowed fryers (fish and chips originated in mid-nineteenth-century Lancashire and London as the marriage of Jewish and Irish immigrant food traditions).[41] Yet for many Britons of diverse social classes and religious and racial backgrounds, fish increasingly means salmon.

Fish are a fixture of Jewish cuisine because they are *pareve* (neither dairy nor meat) and can be eaten with dairy foods or meat. Nor do they have to be ritually slaughtered. The fish that more affluent Jews traditionally ate in inland Eastern Europe were carp and pike; the less well off made do with roach, tench and chub (also salt herring).[42] As Jews fled to Britain and North America, salmon replaced these fish. Smoked salmon (lox) as a Jewish culinary tradition emerged from American immigrant communities at the turn of the twentieth century. (The original lox – the word probably derives from the German for salmon,

Lachs – was not actually smoked. Before refrigeration became widespread, Pacific salmon destined for the delicatessens of east coast cities was packed in barrels of salt brine. On arrival, the salt was soaked off and the fish sliced.) At bat and bar mitzvah, wedding and Sabbath meals, fresh salmon has replaced carp and recipes for eastern Europe's freshwater fish have been adapted. Fresh salmon has even begun to penetrate Britain's Bangladeshi restaurants. Fish, the dietary staple in watery Bangladesh, has rarely featured on menus here. But the award-winning Dundee restaurateur, Abdur Rouf, has gone native by substituting (farmed) salmon for the unobtainable, carp-like freshwater fish, rohi, in his most popular dish, 'Mas Bangla'.

By 2050, most of the fish fried in British fish and chip shops could well be salmon (and a sacred British tradition will live on). In the meantime, a host of novel salmon products are entering the market. In the United States, AquaCuisine carries a range of products made from wild salmon, including salmon burgers and salmon sausages. The pet food company, Arctic Paws, makes a canine treat – salmon jerky – marketed as 'Yummy Chummies'. And in 2004, Domino's Pizza launched a new snack food in Britain – Salmon Bites. A variation on the fish finger, a Salmon Bite consists of 'succulent' flakes of pink-fleshed 'real' salmon. The advertising symbolism of fishermen in a small boat heading out into a remote loch provides a coating of pseudo-authenticity as thick as the casing of tangy lemon and pepper breadcrumbs.

Salmon as a coating for the human body is another kettle of fish. Clothes and salmon are not quite so readily twinned in the popular mind as salmon and food. Nonetheless, sartorial uses continue to evolve alongside ways of eating salmon. The Irish Salmon Skin Leather Company (established in 2000 by John Fitzgerald, a former salmon fisherman from Kerry) offers a range of bags, belts and wallets as well as a dog collar and hip flask. (A leading Irish designer has also fashioned a bustier and miniskirt from Fitzgerald's skins, prompting the headline 'Beauty is skin from the deep'.) Tanning methods for mammal leather are wholly inappropriate for fish skins and Fitzgerald spent two years perfecting the technique at the British School of Leather Technology at University College, Northampton.[43] Fitzgerald, who advised Marion Kite on the conservation of the v&a's Siberian salmon skin gown, draws his inspiration from Irish mythology, at the heart of which resides the 'salmon of knowledge' (see Chapter Six).

The item that has really caught the public eye is the salmon skin leather bikini – a skimpy garment illustrating the endurance of the close relationship between edible and wearable salmon. A leading advocate of regular salmon consumption is Susan Irby, an American celebrity chef ('I love salmon – my favourite food on the planet', she announced in an interview with a bbc local radio station in 2004). Familiar to millions of Americans as 'The Bikini Chef', Irby prepares light and wholesome food conducive to a female figure that looks and feels good in a bikini. To complement the (farmed) Salmon en Papillote over lemon vermicelli and short grain rice that she served a group of diners at London's Athenaeum Hotel on 24 May 2004, she chose a pink bikini made from an Icelandic fish (she owns a pair of matching shoes). A bevy of photographers showed up to snap her sporting her bikini in sunny Hyde Park.

The Bikini Chef is hardly swimming against the current. The London fashion house, skini, has developed an entire range of haute couture salmon leather clothing, from bikinis to jeans. Salmon skin leather is innovative in other ways too. skini's owner and designer, Claudia Escobar, uses skins from processing plants in her native Chile that would otherwise be discarded

'Beauty is skin from the deep': a woman fishing in salmon skin attire crafted by the Irish Salmon Skin Leather Company, which appeared in *The Field* (October 2001).

(she traces her fascination with salmon to childhood fishing trips with her father). Marketed as an eco-friendly alternative to exotic leathers from wild animals such as alligators, salmon skin undergoes a four-week tanning process, during which the natural decay is arrested, the fatty tissues extracted and the

Susan Irby, the
'Bikini Chef', Hyde
Park, London,
May 2004.

Salmon skin jeans from SKINI.

SKINI
London

fishy odour banished. Unlike animal hide, salmon skin enjoys a natural elasticity and 'memory' that retains the wearer's shape; it also dries quickly. In addition, it's lighter, softer and more supple – also stronger and more resistant to scratching and everyday wear and tear. Tensile strength is greater than that of mammal leather because the fish dwells in fresh and salt water (and a salmon leather bikini can be worn in sea and swimming pool alike). Until they bury their noses in salmon skin leather, though, most women are sceptical, unable to shake off the expectation of an off-putting aroma.

Though the quantity of salmon skin we wear on our bodies is unlikely to match the amount of flesh we put into our stomachs, our dependence on the fish has been profound. Nonetheless, we have been making life hard for our beloved salmon for centuries. Judging by the treatment we have meted out, it would appear to be (as Charles Dickens wryly remarked) 'our deadliest enemy instead of our best friend'.[44]

3 Unfortunate Salmon

Charles Kingsley, the nineteenth-century British novelist and keen angler, had never heard of the health benefits of eating fish with substantial amounts of long-chain, unsaturated Omega-3 fatty acids. Still, he rated the noble salmon a peerless dish. 'Of all Heaven's gifts of food', he announced in *The Water-Babies*, 'the one to be protected most carefully is that worthy gentleman salmon, who is generous enough to go down to the sea weighing five ounces, and to come back next year weighing five pounds, without having cost the soil or the state one farthing.'[1] Kingsley's indignation over the ingratitude that those who benefited from its largesse displayed toward the incomparable (Atlantic) salmon fed into a national debate over the fish's future in the 1860s. At this time, regardless of the different species, there was just one sort of salmon: the wild one (broadly defined as a population maintained by natural spawning for at least two full generations). Soon, a second form would be added as a technocratic solution to the salmon's floundering numbers was sought: the semi-wild fish born and raised in a hatchery and eventually released into rivers. Since the 1960s, a third type has emerged and quickly become the dominant variety in the Atlantic world: the fish farm's domestic salmon. A fourth kind has recently been made but is not yet on general release: the genetically modified salmon. Yet in some future scenario, we may revert to just one kind of salmon. This time, though, the sole salmon could be the fourth salmon, an ingenious man-made gift of food. This chapter looks at how we, as a species, have mistreated the first salmon – Kingsley's heaven-sent wonder food – and compromised its watery world.

THE LEAPER'S FALL

Many rivers in northwest Europe once bristled with salmon. The picturesque little wine towns of St Goar, Goarhausen and Bacharach on the scenic gorge of the middle Rhine, for instance, were once thriving salmon villages. These fisheries had dwindled substantially by 1900, however, due to dredging and, on the upper Rhine, dams. Yet postcards still displayed the time-honoured motif of the salmon fisherman tapping the deep pool beneath the hulking mass of the fabled Lorelei.[2] That the Rhine's Swiss headwaters were prime spawning grounds is suggested by the 'Salmon Stübli' (taverns) with their salmon-shaped brass signs in Stein-am-Rhein. And one of Basel's traditional dishes is Saumon à la Baloise – fillets served in a white wine sauce with sautéed Spanish onions.

Saumon à la Baloise, though, is no longer made with local fish. The last Rhine salmon was caught in 1958. And the only major river system in northern and western France that has retained even a residual breeding population is the Loire-Allier. But the squeeze on the fish predates industrialization. A leading English authority on animal husbandry, Leonard Mascall, concluded in 1590 that 'none cares for the preserving of the commonwealth; whereby they cannot increase, nor yet suffer to grow'.[3] Degraded habitat combined with ruthless harvesting placed the fish under considerable stress in early modern times in rivers like the Seine. Organic residues such as manure and the effluent from slaughterhouses, breweries and tanneries de-oxygenated freshwater well before textile mills, steel plants and coal mines contaminated the salmon's environs.

Efforts to alleviate these abuses are as old as the infringements themselves. The desire to protect salmon fisheries precipitated what was possibly the first anti-pollution legislation. In 1466, the Dublin Corporation acted against tanners who washed their leather in the Liffey, imposing a three-quarter pence fine for each offence.[4] Forty-shilling fines for flax manufacturers were decreed in Scotland in 1606 because 'the laying of lint in lochs and burnes is . . . hurtful to all fishes bred within the same'. And according to the provisions of a Scottish act of 1685, millers who captured smolts in creels or raised dams were punishable by a month in prison, irons or stocks, to be fed on bread and water at their own expense.

Heavy industrial pollution delivered the coup de grace. In the mid-1700s, Warrington on the north bank of the Mersey was 'famous for salmon fishing', huge quantities being despatched 180 miles by stagecoach to London twice a week.[5] A century later, a few decades before the first shipments of tinned Pacific salmon were arriving up the river, the Mersey's salmon were practically gone. The Thames, in Izaak Walton's view, produced the best-tasting salmon in England.[6] In the late 1700s, one of the most familiar sights on the bank of the Thames in the village of Barnes, just 13 kilometres upstream from London Bridge, was the salmon fisherman with his net. Yet not a single gleaming salmon on the marble slabs at Billingsgate fish market, Dickens bewailed, was locally caught in 1860. In the fifteenth century, the Westminster Abbey monk, John Flets, had blamed declining numbers in the Thames on divine disapproval following the lapsing of the 'accustomed offering of tithe fish' that fishermen formerly paid to the Abbot of St Peter's,

Westminster (the ministers of riverfront parishes, who wanted their own share, prevented compliance).[7] But Dickens was clear about the basic problem: too many big nets. To convey just how slim the chances of escape were, he drew a vivid analogy:

> Imagine Rotten Row a salmon stream, the good citizens salmon. Four P.M., the spate and the fish running up, a great net is spread at the three arches at Hyde Park–corner, another great net from the statue to the Duke's house, nets half way across the Row every fifty yards . . . add to this, fierce and cunning ogres fishing for us from the walk with rods and hooks baited with devices the most tempting to our nature. How many of us would get up to Kensington Gardens . . . one out of a thousand would get away safely. Rotten Row would soon become depopulated, Kensington Gardens spawnless, and the race extinct; the ogres would give up preserving our race.[8]

Stories abound about the last salmon caught in the Thames. Some claimed it was taken near Maidenhead in 1821. Others related that the final one, a 20-pound (9 kg) fish, was captured near Surly Hall, above Windsor, and sold to King George IV (then living at Virginia Water) for a guinea a pound. (The king apparently sought one, in vain, for his coronation in July 1821.)[9] A rival source brings the solemn occasion forward to 1833 (yet concurs that a monarch, William IV, bought it).[10] Sightings on the lower Thames were reported in 1860 – the first, some claimed, for 20 years. But the river was effectively salmon-less.[11]

'The cry of "Salmon in Danger!" is now resounding throughout the length and breadth of the land', Dickens announced in 1861. He predicted gloomily that 'a few years, a little more overpopulation, a few more tons of factory poison, a few fresh poaching devices and newly-invented contrivances . . . and the salmon will be gone – he will become extinct'.[12] These widely shared concerns had prompted the appointment of a Royal Commission of Inquiry (1860) into the 'Salmon Fisheries of England and Wales, with a view to increasing the supply of a valuable article of food for the public'. The ensuing legislation banned the use of lights and spears (an activity known as 'leistering' – see the next chapter), small-mesh nets and so-called fixed engines (stationary nets); required fish passes for mill dams and gaps in weirs at least a tenth of the stream's width; established closed seasons and catch limits; appointed a board of conservators for each river, and two inspectors for England and Wales.[13]

One of the early inspectors was Frank Buckland, a pioneer in the art of salmon culture (artificial propagation) who characterized his all-consuming vocation as being 'to attend to, and carefully watch, the interests of the King of Fish'.[14] Buckland handstripped eggs and milt from ripe salmon, incubated them in hatcheries and raised the young fish (some of these operations even took place in his own kitchen in central London). Later, when they had reached the alevin and parr stages, he released them into the Thames, hoping to boost the production of young salmon. (Artificial propagation of salmon began on a larger scale with chinooks at a hatchery on California's McCloud River, a tributary of the Sacramento, in 1872.)

To strip their eggs for artificial propagation, salmon are trapped in a hatchery at Astoria, Oregon, 1941.

In the early evening of 18 April 1870, when informed by telegram that a sprat fisherman had netted a female salmon at Gravesend Reach, Buckland thought his efforts had been rewarded (though he was open to the possibility that she was a Dutch salmon that porpoises had diverted from the Rhine). He rushed down to the hotel where she was 'lying in state' on a large pewter dish and the assembled throng (to his horror) was debating how to cook it. He bought this exceedingly beautiful 'treasure' (weighing 10.5 kg and between five and seven years old) for two pounds and six shillings. Having garnished it with seaweed, wrapped it in newspaper, and placed it on a board, he and a friend bore it like a small coffin to the nearest station. On his way home from his local station, Buckland passed the Athenaeum Club and took great pleasure in showing it off to a friend who was sceptical about the Thames's prospects as a rejuvenated salmon river. The next morning, he took his fish to Windsor Castle to show it to a keen fellow angler and naturalist, Prince Christian of Schleswig-Holstein-Sonderburg, husband of Princess Helena Victoria (and Ranger of Windsor Great Park).[15]

The next stop for this overnight piscine celebrity was the Museum of Economic Fish Culture that Buckland had established at the South Kensington Museum (the forerunner of the Science Museum). In addition to a stuffed seagull with a copy of the act of Parliament for the preservation of seabirds in its beak and a mouse trapped by an oyster, the cramped premises featured hatchery apparatus, the equipment needed to transport salmon ova to Australia, a working model of a salmon ladder down which water flowed and up which young salmon swam, and a number of plaster casts of what Buckland called *poissons célèbres* – including a Rhine specimen weighing 31 kilograms.[16]

Though Scotland's salmon rivers remained in better shape than England's or Wales's, pollution blighted even the most renowned waters. Another iconic Scottish product, whisky, was a major culprit. Twenty-seven distilleries sat on the banks of the Spey in the 1890s and an indignant Augustus Grimble relates how he was fishing one day just below Aberlour Burn, where a distillery was sited, when a sudden discharge of 'burnt ale' (a waste product) turned clear water a muddy yellow with 'horrid-looking froth floating on the surface and varying in size from a saucer to the top of a small tea-table'. This concoction was lethal to fry, parr and smolt. Legal action against the distillers, initiated by the Countess Dowager of Seafield, resulted in stiff fines.[17]

In addition to pollution and over-fishing, deforestation and agriculture have contributed to the wild salmon's plight. Denuded soil washes into rivers and ruins the crystal waters and gravel beds of spawning grounds. Erosion also transforms the cool waters of a deep channel with stable banks, good shade and decent pools into a warm, shallow and braided stream. Sheep and cattle exacerbate riverbank erosion, while arable farming aggravates run off. Add the cocktail of farm slurry, silage, chemical fertilizers and the pesticides from sheep dips (which also wipe out the insects on which young salmon subsist) and it is not surprising that rivers flowing through today's post-industrial cities can be considerably cleaner than their rural stretches.

The salmon's European fate was replicated across the Atlantic and, eventually, though by no means as devastatingly, in the Pacific. Whatever the quantities involved might have been before Europeans arrived, North America's Atlantic salmon fisheries were in decline by the 1850s. New England's commercial fishery ended in 1948. Canada's more or less shut down for good in 1998. But the recovery in stocks that many advocates of a ban had predicted has not materialized. For young, post-smolt salmon comparable in size to mackerel, that tend to swim close to the surface, are intercepted en route to their summer feeding grounds by trawlers fishing at the surface for herring, mackerel and blue whiting. Pacific stocks, exploited later, held out longer. At the time of Lewis and Clark, the annual number running up the most important American salmon river – the Columbia – is reckoned to have been between 10 and 15 million.[18] In 1866, when catches on the Columbia were first recorded, 15,000 chinook were taken. By 1870, the number had risen to 367,000. The peak catch was 3.6 million fish in 1918. By the mid-1930s, when the first dams were being erected, numbers had plunged to 1.4 million.

Salmon have faced obstacles in the shape of weirs for centuries. But a string of gargantuan dams such as Bonneville, built for reclamation and hydro-electricity, were an entirely different proposition. The fish ladder (invented in the 1830s) was hailed as a palliative. But big dams (Grand Coulee on the Columbia rears up 150 m) do more than block passage. The reservoirs behind them inundate spawning grounds. The propeller blades of turbines rub off scales and abrade fins. 'Gas bubble disease' killed 5 million fish on the Columbia-Snake in 1971 alone.[19] Young salmon entering the waters behind dams also have difficulty locating the current, resulting in disorientation, wasted energy and, sometimes, failure to migrate. The confused and the delayed often fall prey to the fish that flourish in the still, fetid waters.

The first big dam on the Columbia River, the Bonneville Dam, completed in 1938; 40 miles east of Portland in the Columbia River Gorge.

In the ultimate act of empathy with the damned salmon, four Idahoans (the 'Sockeye Swimmers') swam 724 kilometres down the Salmon and Snake rivers in July 1995 to publicize the ordeal of the juvenile sockeye smolt. Over the Salmon's free-flowing section, they clocked up a brisk 48 kilometres a day. When they entered the orbit of the first dam on the lower Snake, though, their progress stalled. In the 48 kilometres of slack water behind Lower Granite Dam, they managed only ten daily kilometres. Those who march in 'Save-the-Dams' rallies insist that any negative impacts can be readily remedied by installing 'fish-friendly' turbines, barging and trucking young fish around dams, or sending them down a gigantic waterslide called a removable spillway weir. Increasingly, though, the wild salmon's champions urge a more radical solution: removal of dams to restore the river conditions under which the fish have spent virtually their entire evolutionary history.

Human agency is not always responsible, however, for the fish's misfortunes. The cause of the Columbia's disastrous runs of 1877, 1891 and 1926 was El Niño, which temporarily reverses the customary (east to west) direction of surface winds in the

A fish recorder for the United States Army Corps of Engineers looks into a counting station fishway at the Bonneville Dam, c. 1943.

Fish Ladder at the Bonneville Dam on Columbia River, Oregon, 1953. Visitors gaze down from a bridge, in the hope of seeing salmon using the facility designed to allow then to circumvent the massive concrete barrier that blocks their migrations.

equatorial Pacific. By bringing warmer water toward the South American mainland, El Niño interferes with the currents that deliver nutrients from lower levels, encouraging the growth of tiny organisms on which fish feed. The best known consequence is the collapse of the Peruvian anchovy fishery. But on rare occasions (including 1877, 1891 and 1926), El Niño's effects extended to the northeast Pacific, depleting nutrients and bringing summer drought. In addition, warm-water species such as hake flooded north, preying on juvenile salmon. Even as late as the 1920s, virtually nobody outside Peru had heard of El Niño, let alone understood its repercussions. So just as Americans blamed human actions for the precipitous declines associated with these developments – commercial fishermen, sportsmen, Indians and dam operators indulged in a bout of mutual recrimination – they credited artificial propagation for subsequent recoveries. The real explanation, though, was the resumption of normal conditions in the equatorial Pacific. 'Nature', Joseph Taylor explains, 'took away what nature would eventually give back.'[20]

DOWN ON THE FISH FARM

Artificial propagation, as the El Niño episode suggests, was often hailed as a wonder cure. But some advocates were aware of its limits. As early as 1873, Buckland informed *The Times* that the best remedy was to open up 'as many miles of spawning ground as possible', because the fish 'know their own business much better than we do'.[21] Juvenile salmon that had endured a baptism of natural fire were far more street-wise than naïve young hatchery salmon often released far too early. (By the 1910s, young fish were kept in feeding ponds until they stood a better chance of survival. But much of their feed – horse meat,

tripe and condemned pork and beef – was inappropriate and promoted disease.) In a 1992 study comparing their behaviour with that of hatchery fish in an aquarium that simulated a stream, canny wild salmon hugged the edges, retreating to cover after feeding, and swam near the bottom to avoid currents. By contrast, hatchery salmon exposed themselves to predators by swimming near the surface in packs and wasted energy fighting currents. 'A fish that acts that way in the wild', explained researchers, 'is going to be a dead fish.'[22] The disease resistance that wild stocks build up over generations in a particular stream also demonstrates superior 'stream smartness'.

The next loudly trumpeted panacea was the logical extension of artificial propagation: salmon farming. Responding to the demise of its wild stocks in the mid 1960s, Norway pioneered salmon cultivation in floating pens anchored by cables in protected fjords. Since the first Scottish venture at Lochailort (1969), nearly every suitable site on Scotland's west coast has become occupied. Enterprises sprouted up along both Canadian coasts in the early 1980s, but especially in British Columbia. In the early 1990s, this increasingly profitable industry spread to Chile (now, after Norway, the world's largest producer).

But set against the economic benefits – farmed salmon are worth more to the Scottish economy than lamb and beef output combined – are the consequences for their wild counterparts. In the early days, Norwegian and Scottish fish farmers promoted their product as the salvation of remaining Atlantic stocks because it would make commercial fishing unprofitable. They were certainly right about the future of commercial fishing; by 1981, the Atlantic's farmed production had exceeded its commercial catch.[23] But any wild stocks that may have been reprieved as a result have been adversely affected in other ways. Meanwhile, the farmed salmon's own quality of life has become a tendentious issue too.

When they turn into smolt, farmed parr are transferred from freshwater hatcheries to seawater cages. Though hardly the proverbial sardine in a can, each adult (roughly three-quarters of a metre long) has the equivalent of a bath tub of water (according to the Compassion in World Farming Trust). The animal welfare expert, Philip Lymbery, observes that their tendency to circle endlessly in dense shoals 'could well be reminiscent of caged big cats pacing in small zoo pens'.[24]

Diseases and parasites are no strangers to the wild. But packed cages create ideal conditions for their spread in epidemic form. Furunculosis is a fatal affliction characterized by red spots containing bacteria that rot blood vessels and tissue and damage kidneys. Farmed Atlantics of Scottish origin have transmitted it to wild chum migrating past pens in Echo Bay, British Columbia. (Keeping farmed and wild salmon apart has also proved difficult because farmed stock routinely escape their open topped cages during storms and when seals damage the netting.) Farmed salmon afflicted by an even deadlier virus, Infectious Salmon Anaemia (ISA), often betray no external signs of illness apart from lethargy. ISA, which causes haemorrhaging in the liver and kidneys, has no known cure. It thrives in shallow water with high fish densities and an initial outbreak in Scotland in May 1998 resulted in mass disinfections and quarantines and the slaughter of 4 million fish. This calamity generated the first wave of bad publicity for salmon farming in the mainstream British print media. The cover of the satirical magazine, *Punch* (16–29 January 1999), featured the head of a wild spawning male with menacing hook jaw and enlarged teeth, emitting a 'Moo'. The caption read 'Salmon: The New BSE' (a reference to the recent outbreak of so-called mad cow disease). Within a year, ISA had spread to wild salmon. Many farmed salmon, related *Punch*, had become sick and distressed, 'swimming feebly near the bottom of their pens, their eyes bulging and blood-spotted, and their bellies swollen'. The article also hinted at a rather too cosy relationship between government and industry, resulting in a lack of political will to force powerful multinationals that delivered welcome jobs to remote communities to clean up their act.

Punch also raised the question of the transfer of sea lice.[25] Farm escapees communicate the lice that flourish in teeming cages (eating mucus, scales, skin and, sometimes, the flesh itself) to wild salmon (which usually shed their complement on reaching fresh water). The antibiotics, pesticides and fungicides administered in feed to combat diseases and parasites seep into the marine food chain through faeces and excess feed that sinks to the bottom. These pollutants hit shellfish particularly hard but farming disadvantages other members of marine ecosystems in other ways too. In British Columbia, underwater sirens to deter the seals and sea lions that salmon pens attract scare whales from their customary feeding grounds (and may actually be attracting rather than repelling predators – the 'dinner bell effect').

Tremendous quantities of faeces leach into waters where sea-bound wild smolt rest and feed. Natural forces struggle to break down the deluge of ammonia-rich excreta, a problem aggravated by the poor flushing systems of the farms' loch-head locations. Farm filth eventually creates oxygen-depleted 'dead zones' on the sea bed. In his critique of modern food production methods (2001), the veteran BBC broadcaster, John Humphrys, recounts a scuba dive he took in a loch – the site, a year previously, of a salmon farm. There was nothing but a thick carpet of black sludge. As he tries to walk along the bottom on his hands, Humphrys becomes engulfed in a cloud of muck.[26]

Organized opposition in Britain first emerged in the late 1980s through the Campaign for Real Fish. Poor flavour was the initial objection. 'Farmed salmon has a distinctly muddy taste', remarked Egon Ronay (president of the British Academy of Gastronomes), 'whereas wild salmon really tastes like salmon.' A *Sunday Times* article in 1987 referred to the travesties of artificial colouring and 'smoking' by dipping in smoke-flavoured chemicals, and noted calls for labelling to distinguish wild from farmed and to indicate the presence of additives. The feature also decried the sorry state of fish deprived of move-ment in over-crowded pens.[27]

In stark contrast to the fish's popular image, the reality for the vast majority of Atlantic salmon is captivity. The mighty king of fish has fallen to the lowly status of mass-produced liv-ing commodity ridden with disease and chemically dependent ('Wild Salmon Don't Do Drugs' is a bumper sticker slogan pop-ular among commercial fishermen on North America's Pacific coast). Some farmed salmon are also effectively blind (chronic cataracts) and deformed – a condition known as 'humpback',

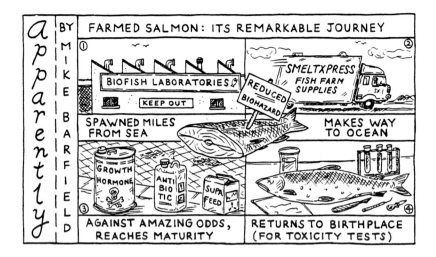

The 'remarkable journey' of farmed salmon, recorded in a *Private Eye* cartoon (6–19 February 2004).

which lends them the appearance of carp rather than the hump-back (pink) salmon and is attributable to the high temperatures applied to incubating ova to hasten hatching.

Those that survive the high mortality rates of caged life bear the marks of incarceration. Farmed escapees can be distinguished from wild *Salmo salar* by examining the tails and fins, which are much smaller due to lack of exercise; the only leaping a farmed salmon does is part of a vain effort to shake off lice. Tails and fins are also frayed and abraded by in-fighting and friction with cage bars. Penned salmon have blunter noses due to close confinement. Critics also publicize the health threat to human consumers from the accumulation of carcinogenic and other toxic substances in farmed salmon. These, they claim, taint breast milk, depress the immune system and affect the neural tissues.[28]

A watchword for critics is authenticity. Supplanting the wild with the farmed, according to Ron Greer, a former scientist at the Scottish Executive's freshwater fisheries research laboratory, is like 'knocking down Edinburgh castle and replacing it with a concrete replica'.[29] For many critics, the hallmark of fakery is the colour of farmed flesh. Whereas the flaming red of the most commercially desirable wild salmon reflects their diet of krill, the farmed fish's hue derives from colourants added to feed. For market research indicates that consumers associate colour with flavour and freshness. Enter the designer salmon. The Swiss pharmaceutical giant, Hoffmann-LaRoche, has devised a colour chart (2003) called the SalmoFan, which resembles the paint charts available at decorating stores. The 33 shades range from bold bubble-gum to a very subtle rose. Just as a young girl can choose her favourite pink tone for her bedroom walls, a salmon farmer can do the same for his fish. Recent Norwegian experiments confirmed consumer preference for the deepest coloured fillets. Consumers, observed the Norwegian Food Research Institute, 'are willing to pay significantly more for salmon fillets with normal, or above normal redness'.[30]

The salmon industry insists that its colourants (it objects to the term dye) are no less natural than the carotenoid pigments in the crustaceans that colour wild salmon. Yet they are synthetically prepared in a laboratory and potentially harmful. Responding to studies indicating that prolonged exposure to canthaxanthin can cause pigments to accumulate on the human retina, the European Union issued a food safety edict in 2003 that imposed a three-fold reduction in the permissible amount in feed. And, whatever we call them – pigments, colourants or dyes – without them farmed flesh would be an unappetizing grey and, therefore, as the Norwegian study concluded, 'difficult to market'.

Salmon farmers believe that consumers would be sick of their product long before it made them sick. Yet controversy persists. American research published in *Science* (9 January

2004) reignited public debate. The authors claimed that amounts of hazardous chemicals such as organochlorine pesticides and dioxins – long-lasting compounds that become concentrated as they move up the food chain – are significantly higher in farmed salmon than in wild. They pinpointed diet as the main reason for the difference.[31] Salmon differ fundamentally from other intensively reared animals in that they are carnivorous. In their aquatic feedlots, these swimming livestock are fed pellets consisting of fish meal, ground up raw fish, and fish oil fortified with vitamins. The fish in question are those usually too small for human consumption (so-called 'industrial' or 'forage' fish) that dwell on the ocean-floor, where they absorb residual toxins before factory ships vacuum them up. Wild salmon are lower in contaminants because they eat smaller, less contaminated creatures like shrimp and krill. (Another bumper sticker from the Pacific Northwest proclaims that 'Real Salmon Don't Eat Pellets'.) In former centuries, employment contracts in Europe stipulated that apprentices and servants should not be fed salmon more than three times a week. Today, some researchers recommend that consumers limit their intake of farmed salmon from certain countries to between three and six portions a year.[32]

To restore public confidence in their battered product, Scottish Quality Salmon, a trade organization representing two-thirds of the Scottish salmon farming industry, launched a £3 million advertising blitz in the British press in July 2004. One advert showed salmon cages floating in a loch as calm as a swimming pool. The impression of a spacious and tranquil setting was reinforced by the information that 98 per cent of a fish pen is occupied by water and that most pens are equivalent in volume to two Olympic-size swimming pools. 'To produce such high quality salmon', ran the caption, 'you must have the right ingredients. Fresh air, clear loch water and great highland views.' 'These unique ingredients', Scottish Quality Salmon proclaimed, 'can only be found in the great surroundings of Scotland.' The second advert, featuring a rugged looking young fish farmer cradling a salmon, sent the message that the fish – and you, the consumer – are in safe hands. The slogan summing up the product was 'Naturally they're the best'.

The Salmon Farm Protest Group quickly contested this claim to naturalness, citing the use of colourants and medicated feeds and the inadvertent presence of toxins. It also challenged the claim of uniqueness on behalf of Scottish farmed salmon. Salmon farming is a global industry based in Norway and Holland. And Scotland's salmon farmers employ the same methods as their counterparts in other countries – where there's also plenty of stunning scenery, fresh air and glorious views.

Whether farmed or wild, oily fish like salmon are the only significant source of Omega-3 fatty acids, which, it has become well known since Kingsley's time, help combat heart disease. Recent studies suggest that these fatty acids can also assist in maintaining optimal brain functioning, fend off Alzheimer's disease and breast cancer and relieve arthritic and menstrual pains. And, according to the very latest claims, they possess anti-depressant qualities, can alleviate dyslexia, hyperactivity and other learning difficulties in children, mitigate the effects of alcohol and tobacco, and protect skin against ultraviolet rays. In view of these touted benefits, many fish eaters feel that the advantages of eating farmed salmon substantially outweigh the risks. In October 2004, a BBC1 series that explored various public fears dedicated an episode to farmed salmon ('Should I Worry About . . . Farmed Salmon'). Having considered the pros and cons, the presenter, Richard Hammond, decided that he would definitely not be worrying. Nor is he alone. Despite a temporary blip early in 2004 in the wake of the *Science* report,

Britons ate 86.4 million salmon meals between March and May 2004, a 20 per cent rise over the same period in 2003.[33]

Farmed salmon are a potential source of biological as well as chemical pollution. Pointing out that farmed stock are bred for rapidity of growth, uniformity of size and passivity (docility is clearly an asset in crowded pens), fish farmers in the early days of their industry pooh-poohed fears that their fish would damage the genetic viability of wild fish through interbreeding. An escapee's survival rate was likely to be minimal, they claimed, because their sheltered existence rendered them easy prey. It transpired, though, that farmed *Salmo salar* was tougher and more adaptable than predicted. 'We were told they wouldn't escape. They escaped', reflected Jennifer Lash, director of the Living Oceans Society, a conservation organization in British Columbia's Broughton Archipelago, in 2001. 'We were told they wouldn't survive in the wild', she continued. 'They survived. We were told they wouldn't get upstream. They got upstream. We were told they wouldn't reproduce. They've reproduced.'[34] Hybridization may erode the wild fish's homing instinct. Some fear that the possibility of a homogenized salmon strain emerging through 'genetic swamping' has been strengthened by the use of the domesticated version of *Salmo salar* as farm stock in British Columbian and Chilean operations.[35] These worries may be overblown, though, for farmed *Salmo salar* seems to be at sea at sea. The stomachs of escapees caught in trawl nets contain less food than those of their wild counterparts while scale analysis suggests that their oceanic growth rate compares badly.[36]

THE ULTIMATE TECHNOLOGICAL SALMON

Though they gain weight faster than their wild counterparts – round-the-clock cage lighting provides a further boost to growth rates – farmed salmon still lag behind their main commercial competitor: broiler chicken. Whereas farmed salmon need a couple of years, poultry arrive on supermarket shelves within six weeks of hatching. The next stage in the making of salmon is therefore approaching. Aqua Bounty Farms (Massachusetts) is gearing up for commercial production of what would be the first genetically modified fish species in North America by applying for a permit to the US Food and Drug Administration.[37] Any approval granted at national level has international implications because the transgenic salmon differs profoundly from all other salmon and might also escape. Containing a growth hormone gene extracted from the chinook salmon, 'super salmon' (or 'frankenfish', as their opponents dub it) can grow two to three times faster than regular farmed salmon. The end product could be a fish eight times bigger than its closest relative.

Those who are cooking up transgenic salmon insist that they will be exclusively female and completely sterile. Subjecting eggs to heat creates an extra (third) set of chromosomes so that females can only produce other females (already common practice in trout farming). The resultant sterility maintains flesh quality (which usually deteriorates with the onset of sexual maturity) and converts feed into flesh more efficiently. GM salmon's pioneers have also devised a cheap and apparently foolproof scanning method to verify sterility in individual triploid fish before they leave the hatchery. But what if a male triploid should slip through the safety net? Transgenic males of inordinate size could displace wild males in the breeding stakes and also hog food supplies. According to the computer modelled 'Trojan Gene Hypothesis', just 60 genetically engineered fish among 60,000 wild fish would bring species extinction within 40 generations. And if we end up with just one salmon type – a sort of McSalmon – should that population itself crash, there will be no salmon of any kind left.

The probability that this terrifying scenario will actually materialize is hard to calculate. After all, the reference point for the Trojan Gene Hypothesis is a fish quite unlike any salmon – the genetically modified medaka. This small freshwater fish from Japan matures in 56 days and breeds daily until it dies. Besides, transgenic salmon accustomed (like farmed salmon) to being fed might prove spectacularly inept at foraging. Even if capable of recognizing a likely meal, they would lack the necessary hunting skills and energy reserves to pursue it.

ORGANIC SALMON

To eliminate the danger of contact between the farmed and the wild, environmentalists urge the adoption of fully contained, solid-wall pens made of concrete or plastic with their own waste collection facilities. Yet only (even more expensive) land-based closed tanks can deliver total genetic security. Meanwhile, others promote what they consider to be the only acceptable face of salmon farming (available since 1999): organically reared fish. Like free range hens, these enjoy more *lebensraum* than conventionally farmed fish (though any form of farming frustrates the migratory instinct). Their cages, as well as being larger, are situated in the more open waters of the Orkney Islands and Shetland, where Atlantic Ocean and North Sea merge; coping with high waves and tidal currents, the fish get a good workout (whereas sea lice suffer). Vigorous exercise develops firmer flesh and lowers saturated fat content. As a result, devotees claim, organically raised salmon tastes much better than conventional farming's flabby product.[38] Open-water location also flushes away excrement and food residues more efficiently.

Extensive as opposed to intensive rearing also obviates the need for pesticides, which organic methods prohibit as well as growth promoters and antibiotics. Small 'cleaner' fish called wrasse are sometimes deployed to nibble off sea lice. Organic standards also prohibit synthetic pigments. Organically farmed salmon flesh is therefore rather pale, though crushed prawn and shrimp shells – the only permitted feed additives – impart some of the pinkness that consumers expect. Nonetheless, organic methods cannot guarantee absolute freedom from toxins. Mercury, for example, is no respecter of any kind of salmon.

THE SALMON'S RETURN (LONG LIVE THE KING)

Not all prospects for salmon are bad, however. In the 1930s, the British novelist Henry Williamson expressed the hope that, despite the pollution of once 'pure' rivers, 'one day salmon will be leaping again in the Thames, that Salmo Salar, the Sea Leaper as the Romans named him, will jump once more in the Pool of London, and play around the piers of the bridges'.[39] Williamson did not live to see the rehabilitation of British rivers, many of which are cleaner now than at any time since the Industrial Revolution. As salmon are an 'indicator' species – the state of a local population being as reliable a yardstick of a river system's general health as any – the demise of Britain's heavy industry has been great news for the fish.

Salmon are leaping again in the River Don in the centre of Sheffield, reinvesting that riverside space, 'Salmon Pastures' (most recently a coal-tipping yard), with meaning for the first time in a century and a half. They have also reappeared in the Mersey, the Clyde and the Tyne.[40] These encouraging developments are mirrored on the continent. The Rhine was nicknamed the Sewer of Europe in the early 1970s but, in 1990, a sizeable salmon was caught in a tributary. The Salm, which gave the fish its name, has not yet been recolonized. But the efforts of a restoration campaign (Salmon 2000) bore fruit in 1994 with evidence of natural reproduction on the Sieg, a direct tributary of the Rhine. The returning fish represent a combination of farm escapees, members of residual populations and strays.

Similar restoration campaigns are underway on the Loire-Allier and across Britain. A group of landowners, anglers and conservationists in southwest England established the Westcountry Rivers Trust in 1994 to grapple with the deep-seated causes of decline in Devon. Fencing off large stretches of riverbank has protected them from trampling livestock and farmers have curbed their use of pesticides and fertilizers near banks to reduce run-off. Obstructions have been removed and streamside woodland thinned to create dappled shade – the optimum conditions for the tiny algae (diatoms) on which fry feed. Still, Williamson's dream remains unfulfilled. A few salmon return to the lower Thames each year. But locks prevent them moving upriver. And even if river conditions could be rendered more or less perfect, this would still be the easy bit. Looking after the salmon's interests in their sprawling oceanic realms presents a much more formidable challenge.

In South Wales, in addition to improving riparian habitat, the Wye and Usk Foundation has bought out the drift netters that operate in the Severn Estuary (1999). This is not only a boon for returning and departing salmon but also good for sport fishermen. Yet others besides sportsmen and commercial fishers have sought a place at the great table to guarantee (and maximize) their slice of the salmon pie. The next two chapters explore how securing, granting, protecting and implementing access to the esteemed salmon has been a deep-seated source of bitter human confrontation.

4 Disputed Salmon

'Under Socialism: Who would get the salmon, and who would get the red-herrings?', inquired Robert Blatchford in a best-selling tract credited with making a hundred converts to the socialist cause in 1890s Britain for every person who was per-suaded by Karl Marx's *Das Kapital*. More to the point, though, was Blatchford's follow-up question: 'Who gets the salmon and who gets the red-herrings now?' Red herring was a very salty and strongly flavoured fish deemed an 'indifferent kind of food' by Charles Elmé Francatelli, Queen Victoria's former maitre d'hotel and chief cook, in his popular 'shilling' cookbook for those of 'comparatively slender means' (1861).[1] Not surprisingly, there were no salmon recipes to complement dishes such as 'Stewed Sheep's Trotters', 'Cow-heel Broth' and 'Baked Cod's Head'. And the types of fish Francatelli recommended for fish pie were skate, dabs, flounders, mackerel and conger eel.

'Is it not true', Blatchford continued, 'that the salmon and all other delicacies are monopolised by the idle, while the coarse food falls to the lot of the worker? Perhaps under Socialism the salmon might be eaten by those who catch it'.[2] In his desire to make political capital, Blatchford overlooked the availability of delicious and nutritious tinned salmon from Alaska and British Columbia – a familiar sight on working-class supper plates within 20 years of Francatelli's cookbook's first appearance. By salmon, Blatchford meant fresh British salmon. (His reference to fishermen being deprived of the fruits of their labour also skated over the fact that the growing popularity of sports fishing meant that many of those eating salmon – however middle and upper class – were also doing the catching.) Nonetheless, Blatchford correctly identified the ownership of salmon as a time-honoured and monumental symbol of inequity.

In Scotland, all salmon fishing rights – whether in sea, estuary or river – originally belonged to the Crown. In many instances, though, the Crown had conveyed them on to individuals via written grants (King David 1's to the newly founded Priory of Urquhart on the Spey in 1124 appears to be the earliest). Ownership in England and Wales was also a royal prerogative frequently sold to favoured interests. This right was typically implemented by erecting a barrier across a river to deflect salmon into a kiddle (which later became 'kettle' – perhaps the origin of the expression, 'kettle of fish', a different or pretty kettle of fish being a kiddle damaged by weeds or raided and disabled by poachers). This arrogation of salmon was a particularly sore point in relations between nobility and monarchy during King John's reign, demonstrating that disputes over salmon have not always aligned the haves against the have-nots. A clause in Magna Carta (1215) confronted obstacles to fish migration: 'All kiddles for the future shall be removed altogether from Thames and Medway, and throughout all England, except upon the seashore'.[3] Yet many hindrances remained in place. Richard the Lionheart eventually relinquished his prerogative to install kiddles on the Thames. Thereafter, royal decrees also specified that weirs, dams and dikes must have a gap in the middle big enough for a well-fed, year-old pig to be rotated without touching the weir with its nose or tail.

Religious folk squabbled over salmon as well as kings and barons. The Abbot of St Peter's, Westminster, extracted a salmon tithe until at least 1382. According to the eleventh-century account of Sulcardus, this dates back to when St Peter (the patron saint of fishermen and fishmongers) came to consecrate the church of Thorney (the abbey's forerunner). The apostle arrived on the opposite bank of the Thames one stormy night and asked a local fisherman, Edricus, to row him across and back again afterwards. In gratitude, St Peter 'repaid his services by a miraculous draught of salmon', informing Edricus that he and his fellow fishermen would always enjoy an abundant supply 'provided they made an offering of every tenth fish' to the new church. During a bitter dispute in 1231 between themselves and the minister of Rotherhithe, Surrey, over payment of the tithe for the fish caught within the minister's parish, the monks of Westminster successfully cited St Peter's grant, claiming that it encompassed all salmon caught between Staines Bridge and Yenlade (Yantlet) Creek near Gravesend (effectively the Mayor of London's jurisdiction).[4]

The early fourteenth century brought the first of many Scottish acts governing the use of a weir called a cruive, which, usually in an estuary, sought to catch fish heading upstream in traps set in its gaps (slaps). A meal (flour) mill serving the Burgh of Inverness in 1474 was shut by royal order because salmon were entering the lade and being killed by the wheel. Closed periods and seasons were another attempted means to secure salmon stocks. About 1220, Alexander I of Scotland enacted the 'Saturday's stoppe' at Perth on the Tay, which decreed that salmon must be allowed free passage from Saturday night to Monday morning and made the taking of spawning fish or smolt a capital offence. Over the next two centuries, English and Scottish salmon streams became subject to various prohibitions on fishing between the Nativity of Our Lady (8 September) and St Martin's Day on 12 November (extended to the Feast of St

Andrew, 30 November, in 1424). Though the amount of enforcement is entirely another matter, this body of laws constitutes one of the earliest efforts to regulate the use of a natural resource.

Salmon may have been monopolized by those that Blatchford dismissed as 'the idle', but the privileged had to work pretty hard to protect their access to this delicacy – and sometimes from the predations of those of comparable status. Long simmering friction between the lairds of Ormidale and Glendaruel in Argyllshire boiled over on the Ruel in 1755. Ormidale, whose property was downstream from his rival's, dammed the Ruel to drive his textile mill. Glendaruel issued an ultimatum for the dam's removal. When Ormidale ignored his communication, Glendaruel sent a second missive protesting that the dam was interfering with salmon ascending to his estate. Failing to gain any satisfaction, Glendaruel sent his men to breach the dam, but Ormidale's entourage promptly mended it. These actions were repeated. Glendaruel, at the end of his tether, duly informed his opponent that he planned to show up at the dam with a force of a hundred men the following morning, and invited him to turn up with an equal number. Ormidale's forces duly appeared and faced Glendaruel's army across the Ruel. The latter moved first, plunging into the river to destroy the dam. The warring parties met in mid-stream, brandishing their cudgels, and 'in a twinkling a terrible struggle was in full swing'. Punches were traded, cudgel blows landed and those remaining on the banks hurled rocks. Loss of life was apparently prevented only by the timely intervention of the local minister. None, though, escaped some injury and the river allegedly ran red to the sea. The dispute was subsequently settled in court. To allow spawning salmon to reach his rival's estate, Ormidale was ordered to erect a fish ladder (consisting of box steps) alongside his dam.[5]

A section of the map of Galway in Ireland drawn in 1584 by the Englishman Barnaby Gooche depicts a fisherman spearing salmon from the Great Bridge. He was probably using a casting spear, which was attached to a rope and hurled at the fish harpoon-style.

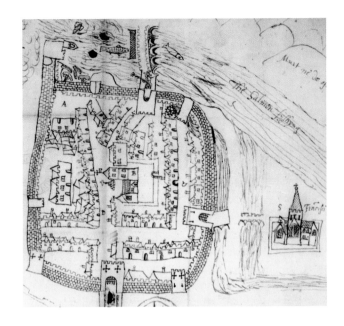

In England and Wales, in contrast to Scotland, the public has the right to fish tidal estuaries and the sea except where the Crown or another party has specifically acquired the right. Spearing is the time-honoured method of catching salmon (legally and illegally) across the British Isles but a venerable form of inter-tidal fishing unique to the River Severn is fishing with putchers. The 1861 Report of the Royal Commission on Salmon Fisheries of England and Wales contained a detailed (if not entirely accurate) description of this 'fixed engine' method, modified little since Saxon times. A putcher is a trumpet-shaped wicker basket of hazel rods and willow hoops, 1.5 to 1.8 metres long, with a mouth 0.6 to 0.9 metres wide. Tapering virtually to a point at the other end to make escape impossible, a putcher resembles a giant ice cream cone. Putchers are arranged in parallel rows stacked up to four high (a rank) on the crossbars of a sturdy wooden frame sometimes 120 metres long and 4 metres high. This frame (which might consist of as many as 500 putchers) is set at a right angle to the shore, the landward end staked at the high water mark with a pole driven into a hole drilled into the flat rocky platforms of the river's bed. (Construction of the second Severn bridge in the early 1990s disclosed traces of several of these stages, some pre-dating the Iron Age.) Many putchers face upstream to catch fish on the ebb tide; salmon swimming 60 centimetres below the surface pass over them at high tide.[6]

The outcome of the commission's investigations, the salmon conservation act of 1861, barred the installation of new fixed engines and reprieved only those in place since 'time immemorial'. Due to their antiquity, few putchers on the Severn were affected. By the 1970s, though their design remained prehistoric, on the west bank, they were increasingly made of wire and plastic and their frames from stainless steel. By century's end, however, as salmon dwindled and anglers gained more clout, the once ubiquitous putcher fisherman had become as

At low tide, George Whitaker tugs a salmon from a putcher at Goldcliff Fisheries on the Welsh bank of the River Severn, 1923.

113

rare as the maker of the split cane fishing rod.[7] The last putcher rank on the Welsh bank worked at Goldcliff Point, Monmouthshire, where the Romans caught salmon to feed their garrisons at Caerleon and Caerwent. Eton College owned the fishing rights between 1451 and 1921 (though it let out the estate and received rent in kind in the form of oxen). Recently, the Wye and Usk Foundation bought out the Goldcliff fishery for five years as part of its efforts to restore these two rivers' spawning populations.

The most ruthlessly efficient method of taking salmon, however, operated on the rivers of North America's west coast in the late nineteenth and early twentieth centuries: the fish wheel. This 'infernal' device, which resembled a fairground Ferris wheel, consisted of compartments of wire gauze that turned with the current and scooped out upstream heading salmon. During his trip up the Columbia, Rudyard Kipling saw many of these voracious contraptions in action. 'Think of the black and bloody murder of it!', he declared, but immediately implicated all his readers: 'you out yonder insist on buying tinned salmon, and the canneries cannot live by letting down lines.'[8]

Fish wheels in Alaska, between c. 1900 and 1916.

An early 19th-century warning to poachers posted by the owners of salmon fishing rights on the River Hodder in north Lancashire.

POACHED SALMON

For those who enjoy legal ownership of the coveted salmon, the most ruthless predator, as already intimated, is often the excluded human. On the early nineteenth-century Tweed in southern Scotland, far from being a solitary and furtive act, poaching was a well-organized, largely overt activity attracting a wide cross-section of the non-gentlemanly community, from shepherds to publicans. Local police and magistrates more or less condoned a practice known as 'burning the waters' that was celebrated in poem, song and novel. Thomas Tod Stoddart of Kelso, one of the Tweed's leading nineteenth-century gentleman anglers, was unwilling to condemn outright a 'manly and vigorous' activity with no commercial purpose that was legitimized by 'immemorial usage'.[9] His collections of angling songs and poems included 'Sonnet – A Reminiscence of Leistering', which was redolent with classical allusions.

115

> A figure stood
> Upon the prow with tall and threatening spear,
> When suddenly in the stream he smote.
> Methought of Charon and his leaky boat;
> Of the torch'd Furies, and of Pluto drear,
> Burning the Stygian tide for lamprey vile[10]

Stoddart also found room for 'The Leisterer's Song', which opens and closes with these stanzas.

> Flashes the blood-red gleam
> Over the midnight slaughter,
> Wild shadows haunt the stream,
> Dark forms glance over the water.
> It is the leisterer's cry!
> A salmon, ho! oho!
> In scales of light the creature bright
> Is glimmering below.

> Rises the cheering shout,
> Over the rapid slaughter;
> The gleaming torches flout
> The old, oak-shadow'd water.
> It is the leisterer's cry!
> The salmon, ho! oho!
> Calmly it lies, and gasps and dies,
> Upon the moss bank low![11]

Salmon are attracted to bright objects; and a torch of burning heather or pine root held over a pool on a dark winter's night revealed all to a considerable depth. The leister was an iron trident with five barbed prongs attached to a five-metre shaft.[12] Parties usually consisted of an oarsman, leisterer and torchbearer/gaffer. By the end of the night's exertions, their backs would be half-frozen and their fronts nearly scorched. Though some poachers wore masks of black crape, leistering was a spectator sport, with much merriment among the hangers on crowding the Tweed's banks.[13]

Walter Scott, who resided on the upper Tweed at Abbotsford, and was an angler and local magistrate to boot, was particularly well qualified to report on this local custom. His historical novel, *Guy Mannering* (1815), contained a heavily romanticized description of the thrilling nocturnal pandemonium that burning the waters entailed.[14] The voraciousness of poaching at the redds, Scott believed, could only be explained by 'a desire to retaliate upon those who engrossed all the fish during the open season, by destroying all such as the close-time throws within the mercy of the high country'.[15] Scott proceeded to explain that landowners and the 'better class of farmers' regarded leistering 'with perfect indifference'. Prosecutions were rare because 'proof of delinquency' was hard to secure in remote country. Officials often colluded too, with leistered salmon sometimes ended up on the dinner tables of unscrupulous water bailiffs. William Scrope, a wealthy landowner who was a friend and neighbour of Scott, related how a bailiff 'sworn to tell of all he saw' blindfolded his eyes before his wife served him an 'illegal' salmon, 'nor was the napkin taken from his eyes till the fins and bones were removed from the room'.[16]

Despite the sporting fraternity's denunciations of poaching and its demise as an organized activity in Scotland by the end of the nineteenth century, illegal fishing retained a fascination for eminent citizens. Inspired by an actual incident in 1897, John Buchan's adventure novel, *John Macnab* (1925), features three middle-aged men from the upper social echelons. Sir Edward

Leithen, Lord Lamancha and Mr John Palliser-Yeates are at the summit of their careers. But they feel strangely and inexplicably unfulfilled and 'stale in mind'. 'Try fishing', Sir Edward's doctor suggests, to which the former attorney general retorts: 'I've killed all the salmon I mean to kill. I never want to look the ugly brutes in the face again.' Exasperated, the doctor recommends the deliberate injection of a frisson of danger into his patient's life. The barrister, budding cabinet minister and banker cook up a lark to restore the flavour to their lives. Signing collectively as 'John Macnab', they write to the owners of three Highland estates, informing them of their plans to poach a stag, a salmon and then another stag. If successful, they undertake to pay £50 to a charity of the estate owners' choice. But if they fail, they agree to pay the proprietors £100. The estates accept the challenge. Sir Edward inevitably draws the lot for the salmon. Disguised as a tramp, the Old Etonian infiltrates his assigned estate and lands a modest eight-pounder. Next morning, a maid at Strathlarrig house discovers a wet parcel on the doorstep. (The other two Macnabs fail to avoid detection but all three are fully cured of their ennui and return to their London lives with renewed zest.)

In Welsh salmon country, tensions peaked on the fabled River Wye in the late 1870s and early 1880s. Armed poachers attacked water bailiffs at Crossgates and stormed the home of an official in Rhayadar. One January night in 1880, after police had failed to arrest a large gang disguised and armed with tridents, reinforcements (issued with cutlasses) were sent into Rhayadar but all they found was a salmon pinned to the door of the market hall; the attached note read: 'Where was the river watchers when I was killed? Where were the police when I was hung there?' On the Edw, a tributary of the Wye, as late as the 1930s,

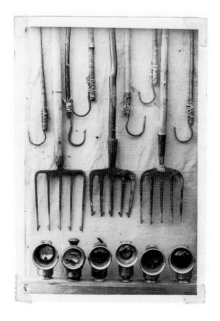

These tools of the poacher's trade – gaffs, barbed forks and lamps – were confiscated from poachers apprehended on the River Ithon in Mid Wales, c. 1910.

119

Salmon-poaching gangs flourished in Mid Wales as late as the 1930s. It was not always a clandestine activity. These masked men were so proud of their large catch, the story goes, that they wanted their picture taken. But the photographer then submitted it to the police as evidence.

gleeful gangs with blackened faces proudly had their pictures taken with their illicit hauls to goad the local law enforcers.

In Scotland and Wales, poaching is mainly the stuff of legend. But it flourishes on the Kamchatka Peninsula, whose rivers host nearly a quarter of the world's Pacific salmon. The Cold War, which effectively sealed off this area as a dedicated military site, keeping at bay for half a century the usual processes of economic development that bring dams, logging and oil and gas extraction, was wonderful for local salmon. Since the Soviet Union's collapse, however, they have been targeted by poachers who supply caviar from chum roe (mainly to Japan). The local economy's deepening dependence on 'red gold' as a way out of the post-Cold War slump was the subject of a TV documentary in November 2004. 'Death Roe' featured a paramilitary helicopter raid on a remote camp, where caviar worth $150,000 was seized from poachers who strip the roe and leave the rest of the fish to rot. (In 2004, Russia established the world's first salmon refuge in southwest Kamchatka, which nominally protects the Kol River from source to sea.)

In North America, access to salmon has been far less restricted than in Britain. Yet resentments against elites rankled here too. Leistering by torchlight, for example, was also popular among mid-nineteenth-century settlers in Lower Canada (Quebec). President Theodore Roosevelt's uncle, one of the growing clique of wealthy American sportsmen who relished salmon fishing in Quebec in the 1860s, believed that leistering ought to have been punishable by death or, at least, life imprisonment.[17] The Pacific coast, though, is where the sparks really flew. If the entrenched interest in Britain was the Crown – entrenched, that is, in the sense of original ownership – here it was the native peoples. According to the Treaty of Neah Bay (1855), in exchange for relinquishing large areas of land, the Makah were guaranteed 'the right of taking fish at all usual and accustomed grounds and stations in common with the citizens of the territory'. This was not so much a grant of rights as the guarantee of rights already possessed. And, at the time, this was not contentious as Euro-American settlers were primarily interested in terrestrial resources. But this changed once the canning industry got into full swing.

Flexing its muscles as a new state in the 1890s, Washington banned various customary means of Indian fishing (snagging, spearing, gaffing and snaring). Indian fishing was further restricted in the name of conservation; their catch might be small in comparison with commercial and sport fishermen's takings, but Indians allegedly hit salmon disproportionately hard by taking spawning stock. Indians could thus be targeted without inconveniencing commercial outfits that harvested salmon before they entered rivers.[18] Blaming Indians fishing with traps in rivers for falling stocks was more palatable politically than tackling the commercial purse seiners and trollers who fished in the sea beyond state jurisdiction, the logging companies that often blocked rivers with the logs they floated downstream or the effluent-discharging pulp and paper mills.

Matters came to a head in the turbulent 1960s, when the 'red power' protest movement added fish-ins to the decade's better known sit-ins, love-ins and be-ins. As salmon runs faded, the state of Washington's fish and game agents used guns, clubs, dogs and tear gas to break up Indian fishing that violated state law. Jane and Peter Fonda, two actors associated with radical causes, joined the fish-ins. But the best known supporter was Marlon Brando, who stood shoulder-to-shoulder with native fishermen on the waterfront. In March 1964, at the mouth of the Puyallup River in Tacoma, Washington, a traditional site closed to Indians since 1907, Brando and the Puyallup tribal leader, Bob Satiacum, were arrested for catching salmon with a driftnet in defiance of state law.

As tensions peaked in the autumn of 1970, the federal government finally intervened. After three years of fact-finding,

Marlon Brando and Bob Satiacum, Puyallup tribal leader, pose with salmon caught in defiance of state laws in the Puyallup River, Washington, just before their arrest. The county prosecutor released Brando without charge.

testimony and deliberation, the senior US district court judge delivered his 203-page decision in February 1974. A sport fisherman with a solid conservative reputation, the elderly George Boldt shocked local white interests (as well as Indians) by not only sustaining treaty rights but defining 'fair and equitable share'. Boldt ruled that Indians should have the opportunity to take up to half of the harvestable catch at their usual and accustomed places, non-treaty fishermen enjoying the same opportunity (using Webster's dictionary of American English, 1828 edition, he ruled that the phrase 'in common with' meant 'divided equally with'). This landmark ruling was informed by the ascendant notion of the Indian as proto-ecologist. 'Religious attitudes and rites', Boldt explained, 'insured that salmon were never wantonly wasted and that water pollution was not permitted during the salmon season.'[19] Outraged white commercial and sports fishermen burnt Boldt in effigy and a witty new bumper sticker appeared: 'Can Judge Boldt'.

Boldt realized that fishing at sea by non-Indians prevented many salmon from reaching those usual and accustomed places (the Indian proportion of the Columbia's catch in the early 1970s was only 5 per cent).[20] Accordingly, he ordered state fish and game authorities to manage salmon populations so that Indians could catch half of the runs that they historically fished.[21] Now that the Indian right to harvest half the available salmon has at last been generally accepted and is finally being enforced, not many salmon, unfortunately, are left for them to harvest.

The Indian fisherman doubtless derives as much pleasure from pursuing his salmon as any white angler. The next chapter takes a closer look, though, at the group with which these joys and thrills are most commonly associated: the sportsman (and sportswoman) for whom the quest for salmon was the most sublime of recreational pursuits.

5 Sporting Salmon

'I have lived!' exclaimed Rudyard Kipling; 'The American Continent may now sink under the sea, for I have taken the best that it yields, and the best was neither dollars, love, nor real estate.' The best that America had to offer was salmon. The day after he observed the Columbia's frenetic canning operations in 1889, Kipling was taken salmon fishing on the Clackamas. Having tasted glory by landing a 5.5 kilogram salmon on a fly after a 37-minute tussle, he made this ecstatic pronouncement (despite his lacerated fingers).[1]

Kipling was not alone in picturing paradise with a salmon river running through it. The ranks of the equally besotted fly fishers include American presidents and British prime ministers, British royalty and American movie stars, industrialists, novelists and celebrities. And not all are male.[2]

Some authorities trace the origins of fly fishing to the River Astraeus in third-century Macedonia (where trout was the quarry). The first rods, made of hazel shoots, were relatively short at about two metres. The fixed lines, roughly the same length, were fashioned from knotted horsehair. This method spread across Europe and vied with the spear as the preferred implement of the common folk for catching pike and carp as well as salmon and trout.[3] The longer rod (often jointed and perhaps extending to just over four metres) and line (though

A small boy looks up to a large chinook salmon, hailed as 'Oregon's finest food fish' in this photograph (taken *c.* 1928) that featured on the cover of the 1984–85 Biennial Report of the Oregon state Department of Fish and Wildlife.

The Marquise de los Agnes Valentia (Viscount Annesley) and his party display their catch from the River Wye in Builth Wells, Powys, in the summer of 1925.

still fixed and hand-made from horsehair) appeared in late medieval times. This was probably the kind used by the author of what is generally considered to be the first celebration in English of fishing for salmon with rod, line and feathered hook: *A Treatyse of Fysshynge wyth an Angle* (published in 1496 as part of the second edition of *The Boke of St Albans*). The author's identity has never been established definitively, but the most popular choice is Dame Juliana Berners (Barnes), prioress of the Benedictine nunnery of Sopwell, near St Albans. Hailing the 'samon' as a 'more statelye fysshe that any man maye angle to in fresshe water', she proceeded to give detailed instructions for catching one (no mean feat given the rudimentary state of the available equipment): 'The Samon is a gentyll fysshe, but he is cumberous for to take. For commo[n]ly he is but in depe places of great ryuers, and for the moste part he holdeth him in the myddes of it, that a man may not come at hym'.[4]

Major pre-industrial advances in fishing technology appeared in the mid-seventeenth century – the era of Izaak Walton (1593–1683).[5] While some lines remained fixed, others

Selection of hand-tied Atlantic salmon flies (mostly hairwing type, including cossebooms, an undertaker, a copper killer, and a green machine).

were threaded through loops screwed into the tip of a rod. The end of the line was hand-held or, increasingly, wound around a reel clipped to the butt of the rod (usually made of bamboo cane). This permitted a superior and longer cast. Flies were also becoming more sophisticated, varied and colourful (and exotic in terms of the raw materials from which they were assembled – not least a staggering range of feathers from macaw to peacock). Running rings supplemented the tip ring on rods by the late 1600s (though they often popped off when the angler was playing a fish). Jointed rods with top sections of bamboo were generally available by the mid-eighteenth century. Industrialization brought ready-made flies, manufactured lines and tackle dealers to sell them.[6]

Fly fishing by non-residents really took off on British rivers in the 1840s and 1850s, thanks to royal example and facilitated by the expanding railway network. Prince Albert and Queen

L. Haghe's water-colour *Ascertaining the Weight*, shows retainers weighing up a gentleman's catch; from William Scrope, *Days and Nights of Salmon Fishing on the Tweed* (1843).

Victoria started spending their summer holidays salmon fishing in the Scottish Highlands in the early 1840s and the landed aristocracy who followed their lead were, in turn, emulated by the new moneyed class of industrialists and financiers who adopted this leisure pursuit as part of their quest for social respectability. The most accessible Scottish river, the Tweed, was a particularly popular destination. By the 1850s, the locals who fished for a living or to supplement their protein supply could no longer afford the rents that English gentry and industrialists were prepared to pay.[7] The visiting angler typically came armed with a five-metre jointed rod of ash, hickory, bamboo or greenheart with a whalebone tip and brass joints, a reel (American makes were the most swish) and a line more likely to have been braided silk than horsehair. (Fibre-glass rods, nylon line and rubber waders were still a long way off.)

These Victorian Britons were convinced that their relationship with the sport was special. 'A plant – as it were – of pure English growth.' This is how a guide to salmon fishing in Norway (1848) hailed the sportsman, who supplied further proof of British superiority over their French neighbours. For 'who ever heard of a Frenchman travelling some twelve or fifteen hundred miles for the avowed purpose of catching Salmon?'[8] British anglers felt just as strongly that the salmon was peculiarly British in its rugged resolution and refusal to say die: 'he will charge the fierce and boiling stream, he will rush at a cataract like a thorough-bred steeple-chase horse, returning to the charge over and over again, like a true British fish as he is'.[9]

The Victorian salmon angler's world was unashamedly exclusive as well as chauvinistic. He oozed distain for the tourist angler as well as the French – the 'Arrys' who 'leave unpleasant souvenirs of their visits in the shape of lunch papers and perhaps small heaps of broken bottles for good dogs to gallop

over!'[10] The monarch of the glen – as Sir Edwin Landseer dubbed the stag in his iconic painting (1851) for the labels of John Dewar's whisky – thus had its aquatic counterpart in the 'monarch of the loch' and the 'monarch of our rivers'.[11] The king of fish was also the king's fish. Balmoral in Aberdeenshire, the royal family's Scottish seat that Albert acquired for Victoria in 1852, includes 24 kilometres of prime fishing on the Dee's south bank. Victoria, Edward VII and George V were all keen salmon anglers. So is Prince Charles ('You may not have fished yourself, to do so for salmon is immensely exciting', he wrote from Balmoral to the tinned salmon-preferring Prime Minister, Harold Wilson, in September 1969.)[12] The most famous royal fisher, though, was Elizabeth the Queen Mother (1900–2001). Fly fishing for salmon was her favourite pastime.

Nineteenth-century paeans abound. The Scottish poem, 'The Taking of the Salmon', well-known on the Tweed, opens with these two stanzas:

A birr! A whirr! – a salmon's on,
A goodly fish! a thumper!

In the preface to *The Salmon Fisher* (1890), the American sportsman Charles Hallock confessed to having 'prigged' this vignette of a gillie gaffing a salmon from the menu card of the Fly-fishers' Club of London on 11 December 1889. He described this menu card image as 'the only truly correct representation of the fact that I have ever seen'.

GAFFING A SALMON.

Bring up, bring up, the ready gaff,
And if we land him, we shall quaff
Another glorious bumper!

Hark! 'tis the music of the reel,
The strong, the quick, the steady;
The line darts from the active wheel,
Have all things right and ready.

and closes with these two:

No birr! No whir! The salmon's ours,
The noble fish – the thumper;
Strike through his gill the ready gaff,
And bending homewards, we shall quaff
Another glorious bumper!

130

Hark! To the music of the reel
We listen with devotion,
There's something in that circling wheel
That wakes the heart's emotion.[13]

One of those whose emotions fly fishing never failed to awaken was Sir Humphry Davy (1778–1829). The English chemist who discovered the anaesthetic qualities of nitrous oxide (laughing gas) is best known as the inventor of the miner's safety lamp. Yet he was also an inveterate angler. Writing a book about his consummate passion supplied a welcome diversion from pain and misery at a time when he was seriously ill and 'wholly incapable of attending to more useful studies'.[14] *Salmonia; or Days of Fly Fishing* mimicked the format and conversational tone of Walton's *Compleat Angler* (though his friend, Walter Scott, regarded it as more factually reliable and informed by broader experience). An 'accomplished' fly fisherman (Halieus) replies to and refutes a friend's objections to angling – not least its cruelty (arguing that the nervous systems of cold-blooded creatures are less sensitive than those of mammals). Then, having converted him, Halieus instructs in the art. Walton, in Scott's view, lacked vision and a sense of adventure, *Compleat Angler* giving the impression of 'a most cockney-like character, and we no more expect Piscator to soar beyond it, and to kill, for example, a salmon of twenty pounds weight with a single hair, than we would look to see his brother linen-draper, John Gilpin, leading a charge of hussars'. In fact, Scott doubted that Walton had ever seen a live salmon.[15] Whereas Walton had not ventured far beyond London, Davy struck as far north as the hallowed Tweed, where he reputedly landed a 19-kilogram salmon above Yair Bridge.

For Scott, nothing came close to this particular sport:

> It requires a dexterous hand and an acute eye to raise and strike [the king of the fish], and when this is achieved the sport is only begun, at the point where, even in trout angling, unless in case of an unusually lively and strong fish, it is at once commenced and ended. Indeed, the most sprightly trout that ever was hooked shows mere child's play in comparison to a fresh-run salmon . . . The pleasure and the suspense are of twenty times the duration – the address and strength required infinitely greater – the prize, when attained, not only more honourable, but more valuable.[16]

Alexander Russel, editor of *The Scotsman*, Scotland's leading newspaper, acknowledged the ostensible foolishness of the exercise in his effort to explain its appeal in the 1860s. 'Look at that otherwise sensible and respectable person, standing midway in the gelid Tweed . . . his shoulders aching, his teeth chittering, his coat-tails afloat, his basket empty. A few hours ago probably, he left a comfortable home, pressing business, waiting clients, and a dinner engagement.' Why? Because, Russel continued, men 'not ignorant of any of the delights to which flesh has served itself heir' were convinced that 'the thrill of joy, fear, and surprise . . . induced by the first *tug* of a salmon, is the most exquisite sensation of which this mortal frame is susceptible'.[17]

Given the intensity of these feelings, the urge to transplant these pleasures to Australia and New Zealand was irresistible. A newspaper in Melbourne, *The Age* (2 April 1858), placed the salmon at the centre of a grand acclimatization plan to render the province of Victoria more familiar to British settlers, hoping 'to see the horse-chestnut and the oak add grandeur and variety to our woods . . . to hear the nightingale singing in our moonlight as

Salmon priest: the lead-headed cosh is so named because it was used to deliver the last rites to a fish that had been landed.

in that of Devonshire, to behold the salmon leaping in our streams as in those of Connemara or Athol'.[18] Sir James Arndell Youl, a prominent Tasmanian colonist, devised the method for successful transmission of ova; by placing the eggs on charcoal and living moss in perforated wooden boxes under ice, they could be kept alive for a hundred days. The clipper *Norfolk* left London in January 1864 with 18,000 salmon ova. The first successful shipment from Britain took place later that year (100,000 salmon ova that Buckland collected from the wild). California rivers were also a source of transplants. But the first shipment from the Country Club of San Francisco to Melbourne, Victoria, also in 1874, was a fiasco. The packing ice melted en route, the eggs hatched and the fish died in a 'putrid mass'.[19]

THE NORWEGIAN ATTRACTION

Davy's 'Halieus' had fished in Norway and Sweden but Scottish streams were good enough for him.[20] By the 1830s, though, an English angler explained, salmon fishing had become such a popular sport that 'the ancient haunts within the British dominions no longer suffice'. And even a piscatorial patriot like Halieus had noted that renowned Scottish rivers were not what they used to be. The intrepid angler's new frontier was Scandinavia, which produced few of its own anglers. The pioneers were Lewis Lloyd and William Bilton (a.k.a. Belton). Captain Lloyd, who his editor hailed as 'a fine specimen of the English gentleman', spent two years roaming Scandinavia in the 1820s. He thrilled to the prowess of Norwegian spawning males, who apparently charged one another with such force that the weaker adversary was sometimes tossed out of the water. Some of the fish to be caught in Norwegian rivers, he insisted, were the size of porpoises.[21] *Two Summers in Norway,*

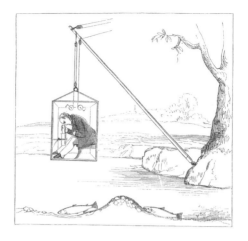

Bilton's account of his exploits in 1837 and 1839, was the first to popularize Norway's premier salmon river, the Namsen. Despite the rigours of the journey and the 'unaccustomed frugality of Norwegian fare, and the want of usual comforts', Bilton (a reverend) maintained it was well worth the effort.[22] A clutch of guides followed the first, and most widely read, *Jones's Guide to Norway, and Salmon Fisher's Pocket Companion* (1848). Written for the 'wandering Walton in a Foreign Land', it hailed Norway as an 'unrivalled' 'fluvial paradise'.[23]

These guides were highly effective publicizing tools, but the likes of the Dukes of Marlborough, Roxburgh and Westminster did not want to rough it in the style of Lewis. So they built sumptuously outfitted and provisioned lodges. Colonel Frank Dugdale of Wroxall Abbey (Warwickshire), who fished on the Namsen at Moum between the early 1880s and 1900s, had one of the most substantial and attractive of these lodges built in an English style in 1891. The golden age of the so-called 'lords' rivers' ended with World War I. After 1919, most aristocrats

were too impoverished and/or heavily taxed to afford these excursions. Industrialists (especially munitions manufacturers) and bankers who had superseded them in wealth sometimes took over their leases. Reports that mixed nostalgia with grumbling were a frequent feature of post-war angling magazines. One disgruntled author, who first fished Norwegian rivers in 1870, complained that rents were now at 'Scotch level' and the fishing mostly 'indifferent'.[24]

While British anglers were discovering Norwegian rivers, Canada's had also started to teem with fly fishermen. Salmon angling was the chief recreational pursuit for British colonial officials and military officers in eastern Canada. They were soon joined by American industrialists who formed the backbone of prestigious clubs that sprouted up on the region's rivers and secured exclusive fishing rights. The oldest and most exclusive, the Restigouche Salmon Club, was founded in Matapedia by nine Americans in 1880. These clubs were sufficiently affluent to

John Singer Sargent, *On His Holidays*, painted in 1901. Alexander, the 14-year old son of Singer's American patron George McCulloch, relaxes after salmon fishing in Norway.

snap up riverfront acreage adjacent to the best pools and to pay farmers not to fish in streams that ran through their farms. They also hired their own wardens. Nonetheless, organized poaching was a huge problem on some Canadian rivers and government officials struggled to maintain order. As in mid Wales, the homes and barns of wardens were burnt down in the 1890s. One particularly ugly confrontation in 1888 between leisterers and out-of-town anglers culminated in the death of an American sport fisher. In many rural areas where arable farming yielded a poor return – as in Scotland – convictions were hard to secure as magistrates often sided with their friends and neighbours against outsiders who were usurping their basic entitlement to take salmon for their immediate needs. In the case of the dead American, the jury returned a verdict of manslaughter.[25]

THE POLITICIAN'S RELEASE

One of the most obscure late nineteenth-century American presidents, Chester Arthur, held the record (23 kg) for a salmon caught on a fly along a stretch of Quebec's Cascapedia River. So many presidents have been so enamoured of angling that Bill Maree has been able to write a 270-page book on the subject. As Maree explains, angling (for fish ranging from 'lordly salmon to the lowly perch') was a peerless way of escaping the pressures of the job.[26] Harry Truman, Dwight Eisenhower, Jimmy Carter and George Bush, Sr were passionate salmon anglers. So was Calvin Coolidge – a decidedly cold fish in most other respects. Yet the most famous salmon fisherman to occupy the White House was Coolidge's successor in the late 1920s, Herbert Hoover. As Secretary of Commerce in the two previous Republican administrations, he worked hard to protect Alaska's salmon stocks from overfishing. He also served as honorary president of the newly formed Izaak Walton League of America (1922), an angler's organization that campaigned for the conservation of fish habitat. For Hoover, angling was anything but exclusive. On the contrary, the inalienable right of all Americans to life, liberty and the pursuit of happiness included – self-evidently, in his view – the pursuit of fish.[27] Angling was also a supremely democratic pursuit because, before the fish, all anglers stood equal. And, no less importantly, there was nothing more ennobling than fishing.

Hoover was accustomed to receiving gifts of salmon. During his tenure at Commerce, canners regularly sent him fresh specimens from Alaska. But his favourite offering came from the Penobscot Salmon Club of Bangor, Maine, the nation's first salmon fishing club. Since 1912, the club's directors had tradi-

President Herbert Hoover is presented with his gift of the first salmon of the 1931 season caught in Bangor Pool on the Penobscot River, Maine.

tionally delivered to the White House the first spring salmon that a club member caught in the Bangor Salmon Pool.[28] The photographs taken on the White House lawns to mark these solemn occasions adorned the walls of the club headquarters, high above the Penobscot River overlooking the aforementioned Pool. There was a major hitch in the normally smooth running of this annual ritual during Hoover's first year in office (1929). As Hoover explained, a 'new and uninformed' White House official sent the fish straight to the kitchen, where the cook immediately prepared it for the oven. In a bid to rescue the day, the cook sewed the head and tail back on and stuffed the fish with cotton. Still, there was something fishy about the photographs if you looked closely.[29] In the late 1930s, this bipartisan tradition broke down, if temporarily, under the pressure of intense political polarization. In 1938, Penobscot club member Sylvia Ross, a Republican stalwart hostile to the New Deal and its chief architect, was so upset at the prospect of the first salmon landing on Franklin D. Roosevelt's dinner table that she paid top dollar to ensure that it did not reach the White House that year.[30]

THE FEMALE TOUCH: WOMEN IN RUBBER[31]

'We have, indeed, often thought', reflected Walter Scott in his review of Davy's *Salmonia*, 'that angling alone offers to man the degree of half-business, half-idleness, which the fair sex find in their needle-work or knitting, which, employing the hands, leaves the mind at liberty, and occupying the attention so far as is necessary to remove the painful sense of a vacuity, yet yields room for contemplation, whether upon things heavenly or earthly, cheerful or melancholy.'[32] Yet women anglers were not unheard of in Victorian times, for, as another authority pointed

out in 1871, 'sex forms no barrier'.[33] And in the early twentieth century, a woman who had traded her knitting needles for a rod and hook showered herself with glory. One of the most celebrated beats on the Tay is Glen Delvine. Here, on 7 October 1922, Miss Georgina Ballantine (using a spinner and rod from P. D. Malloch's store) landed what remains the UK's record for a rod-caught salmon (also the largest fish ever landed in British freshwater). The fish weighed over 29 kilograms and measured 1.37 metres; its girth was 72 centimetres, its head 30 centimetres long and its tail just under that at 28 centimetres.[34] The cast is on display in Perth's museum and art gallery. Underneath is Miss Ballantine's own, understated account of her feat. She was not a member of the original fishing party that Saturday, joining only after someone dropped out. She had already caught three salmon of a respectable size (11, 9.5 and 7.7 kg) from the boat that her father was rowing when the light started to fade. At 6.15 p.m., as the sun was descending behind Birnham Hill, she made one last cast. What was clearly a very powerful fish seized her bait. After a contest that lasted two hours and five minutes – and left her with a cut forefinger as she tried to check the line – she landed the whopper half a mile downstream in pitch blackness. A reading of his scales indicated that he had spent two years in freshwater and three years at sea before returning to the Tay. After posing for pictures with her fish, and once Malloch had made a cast, she donated it to the Perth Royal Infirmary, where it was 'relished by both patients and staff'.[35]

In fact, women hold all the British records for rod-caught salmon.[36] In the late 1930s, a male angler ventured an explanation. Women were far more patient and sometimes bested men in strength and stamina (many male anglers had refused to accept that Miss Ballantine's father, despite his protestations, had not assisted her). Ultimately, though, the explanation was self-evident, consonant with a well-worn gender stereotype: 'women may be presumed to be specially fitted to practice successfully all the arts and artifices necessary to lure, cajole, entice, cozen little and big fish to her hook'.[37]

The opportunities for women to demonstrate their so-called feminine wiles are shrinking, though. The White House received its last Penobscot salmon in 1994 and less than a thousand currently return to that river, compared to 70,000 two centuries ago. Yet the Penobscot is considered the last best chance for restoring a healthy run of *Salmo salar* to an American river. An encouraging sign, in 2003, was an agreement to remove a string of hydro-electric dams.

THE SALMON'S BEST FRIEND

Major Kenneth Dawson of Devon dedicated his 1928 book on local salmon and trout to the fish 'which has given me many of the best days . . . of my life'.[38] In return, anglers have tried to give the salmon something back: respect and a healthy future. Angling in Scotland remains steeped in ritual. At the village of Kenmore, where the Tay flows out of Loch Tay, a ceremony marks the first day of the season in January. A parade, led by a pipe band and celebrity anglers such as the broadcaster Fiona Armstrong, heads from the Kenmore Hotel to the river. When they get there, the salmon and the river are toasted by pouring a quaich of whisky over a boat. The season's end is also marked ceremonially.[39]

Securing the Atlantic salmon's future requires more than respectful ritual, however. Buying out the last drift netting operations may be the best bet for saving and restoring the salmon. Drift nets, which extend miles, are invisible and have tiny mesh. Salmon returning to their natal streams stand little chance of avoiding them. In 2003, the Atlantic Salmon Fund, an international organization founded by Orri Vigfusson, an Icelandic vodka magnate, bought out the last remaining drift netting operations in northeast England to revive the Dee's and the Tweed's stocks. Vigfusson's goal is to restore salmon populations in great European rivers such as the Loire and Rhine to what they were two centuries ago.

Casting a fly on the River Wye, early 21st century.

In economic terms, a salmon caught by a sportsman (who often releases it unharmed) is worth umpteen times more than one caught in a drift net. In the meantime, though, the sport fishing business in regions such as Scotland's west coast is virtually dead. Loch Maree, Wester Ross, was such a fabled destination for salmon (and sea trout) anglers that Davy's alter ego, Halieus, gives a enraptured account of landing a hallowed fish in the River Ewe that connects the loch to the sea.[40] Half a century later, the fishing was still so good that Queen Victoria spent a week of September 1877 at the Loch Maree Hotel. Now, there are more salmon on the walls in the Gillies Bar than in the water. In Connemara, Ireland, Ballynahinch Castle Hotel has also been badly hit. Local wild salmon (and sea trout) populations have disintegrated, due partly to lice infection from nearby farms (though drift netting doubtless aggravates the predicament). The salmon's monetary value to a local economy is one thing. Its larger value is something else. Taking one of the noblest of creatures and converting it into livestock, claimed Patrick O'Flaherty, the hotel's general manager in 2003, 'goes against everything that is natural'.[41] This begs a bigger question, not just for salmon history but for our relations with the rest of nature as a whole: what exactly does it mean to be natural? I shall revisit this question in the conclusion, after considering another aspect of the salmon's value: its cultural currency – expressed in ceremony, myth, visual art, modern western literature and sculpture – for the peoples who co-inhabit its world.

6 Cultural Salmon

Let others praise the herring, the tunny, trout or whale,
Give me the noble salmon with lightning in his tail
(Donagh MacDonagh) [1]

For all the fulsomeness of Irish poet Donagh MacDonagh's eulogy, Thomas Tod Stoddart's paean to the salmon is hard to beat. 'Among objects closely associated with the sublime and beautiful', he raved, 'I cannot help classing the noble fish.' 'The elegance of its form, the justness of its proportions, its glittering and gorgeous apparel', he continued, 'all entitle it to rank loftily in the scale of beauty, while its size and noble bearing, its strength and velocity, the rocks, torrents, and whirlpools among which it glides familiar, unite, in some degree, to elevate its pretentions and give it place withal amid creations of sublimity.' Among members of the 'finny tribe', the salmon was peerless: 'The dolphin, famed in poetry . . . the amulet, carp . . . sturgeon . . . all yield before it the submissive palm.'[2]

Salmon have thoroughly permeated the cultures of north Atlantic and north Pacific. Just as they are critical to the ecological making of place in their role as a keystone species that provides the nutrient base for fellow creatures and forest, they are also central to the cultural making of place. Reflecting the fish's deep, centuries-old local meaning, public houses along Britain's salmon rivers bear names like 'The Leaping Salmon' or depict the fish on their signs. They also appear on postage stamps. Salmon motifs also adorn the coats of arms of many British families and towns. Three salmon pointing upwards are the

The sign of the Bear Hotel in Crickhowell, Mid Wales, shows a bear holding a salmon he has presumably caught in the nearby River Usk.

ensign of the Gloucester and Ord families on the Severn and Tweed respectively. The civic crest of Glasgow (which features a salmon with a gold ring in its mouth) indicates that the Clyde was once a bountiful salmon river.[3] And the motto of the royal burgh of Peebles, at the confluence of the Tweed and the Eddlestone, acknowledges the largesse derived from the fish that swim past toward their redds: 'Increase by Swimming against the Flood' (*Contra nando incrementum*).[4] Meanwhile, the town's arms depict two salmon: one swimming upstream and two heading downriver. Comparable cultural reference points dot northern Europe too. In Germany, elaborate salmon insignia feature on the crests of the Princes of Upper and Lower Salm in the vicinity of the river that gave the fish its name.

A 1959 postage stamp from the Soviet Union shows a chum salmon diving downwards.

A 1956 US postage stamp promoting wildlife conservation depicts a leaping king salmon.

The Heraldic Salmon 1: The crest of the Princes of Upper Salm, Lorraine, includes four salmon. The families from which the princes were descended lived on a tributary of the Moselle river, from which the fish may have derived its name.

The Heraldic Salmon 2: The crest of the Knight family of the city of Gloucester is unusual in showing a cross-section of a salmon, held aloft in complementary fashion by a section of an arm.

The coat of arms of the city of Glasgow.

Over in North America, the fish's lofty cultural profile is initially visible in Newfoundland. Where Salmon Cove Brook empties into the sea near Champney's East, a large island resembles the head of a man lying face up in the water. According to a legend of the Beothucks, the region's indigenous peoples, this is the warrior spirit of Ougen Pushaman ('stone man'). Each year, salmon (*wasemook*) returned to the creek to spawn, ensuring a generous food supply until European settlers snared the fish with massive nets at the river's mouth. Facing imminent starvation, the Beothucks called on the Good Spirit, who despatched a huge warrior. Emerging from the sea, the giant crushed the offending nets and frightened off the intrusive fishermen. Mission accomplished, he lay down and turned to stone.[5]

On the west coast, salmon often enjoy a folkloric association with Coyote, an animal with peerless magical powers. Northwest coastal tribes believed that 'the trickster' taught them how to make traps and spears to catch the salmon he put in their rivers. An Okanagon tribal tale relates how Coyote elevated the salmon to the chief of the fishes (just as he made the grizzly the ruler of the four-footed animals and the eagle the lord of the birds).[6] Coyote was even responsible for making it swim upstream to spawn. Striking a deal with the bears that had difficulty catching the slippery fish as they returned to the sea after spawning, the hungry Coyote persuaded the salmon that they would find a far safer place with soft golden sands to lay their eggs if they swam further up beyond a high falls. At the falls, the bears found it much easier to snatch them and paid a tithe in salmon to Coyote.

The eruption of Mount Shasta, a volcano in northern California, was also attributed to Coyote's taste for salmon. His village had no access to salmon but the nearby Shasta Indians trapped plenty at their weir. These selfless neighbours told the lazy Coyote he could have as many fish as he could carry. While taking a nap on the way home, Coyote's salmon were devoured by a swarm of wasps (yellow jackets), which left nothing but a pile of bones. Coyote returned to the dam and the fearful villagers reluctantly allowed him to take a second load. But the same thing happened. Once again, the Indians took pity on him and also agreed to help protect his third load. They too were powerless to prevent the wasps' raid. All they could do was pursue the insects, which made a bee-line for Mount Shasta's summit, where they disappeared into the top with the stolen salmon. Coyote and the Indians tried to smoke them out with a huge fire that culminated in a massive explosion which spewed the salmon – ready smoked – out of the mountain top (another ending gives the wasps the last laugh: they keep their salmon, pronouncing smoked salmon far superior to dried).[7]

In a Chinook tale from the mouth of the Columbia that the ethnologist Franz Boas recorded in the 1920s, Coyote eventually learns to pay due respect to salmon and instructs humans to follow suit. One day, he spears a salmon, which he cuts up, steams and eats. He goes fishing again next day but without luck. Coyote defecates and asks his excrement why the salmon have gone. Amazed at Coyote's stupidity, his faeces reminds him that the first salmon must be split and roasted. Determined to make amends, Coyote goes fishing again and spears three salmon, which he roasts on spits. The following day, though, the fish have once more disappeared. Again, he relieves his bowels and seeks an explanation from his bodily waste, which explains that he must use separate spits for roasting the head, the back, the roe and the body. Next morning, the fishing is good again, but Coyote commits an almost endless series of further transgressions, among them: failure to roast all his catch before retiring for the night; failure to observe different methods of roasting different species; failure to roast and eat salmon at the same place; failure to throw a salmon from a net to the beach with its head facing upwards; and failure to realize that taboos on opposite banks of a river may be very different. Having finally learnt how to treat salmon correctly, he commands the local people of Clatsop to honour these taboos. He also instructs them that murderers, undertakers, girls entering puberty, menstruating women, widows and widowers must not eat salmon.[8]

Pacific tribes thus observed rituals to ensure the salmon's perennial return. Within the parallel but joined worlds in which people and animals lived, the salmon held the status of 'swimming person', and, like other non-human persons, entered into contractual agreements with its human partners. An animal gave itself as a gift but expected to be treated with respect. If people did not fulfil their obligations, consequences would be dire.

Salmon were supernatural beings living in five big houses under the sea that corresponded to the five Pacific species. Here they assumed human form. Each year, though, at the salmon king's behest, they donned silver skins and went to the human world. Coastal tribes ate their salmon plain but often garnished it with ritual in gratitude. In the 1920s, anthropologist Erna Gunther described various manifestations. The Tsimshian people summoned four ancient shamans to the fisherman's platform when the first salmon was caught. One shaman dressed up in fisherman's clothing and took a rattle in his right hand and an eagle's tail feathers in his left. The shamans then placed the salmon on a mat of fresh cedar bark and, each carrying a corner, transported it to the chief's house led by the one dressed as a fisherman. The rest of the village's shamans, in full regalia, followed them into the house. After depositing the fish on a cedar board, they marched around it four times. Then the fisherman shaman invited two of the oldest shamans to slice up the fish. First, they severed the head. Then they cut off the tail with a knife made from mussel shell.[9] (If a knife of stone or metal were used, it would provoke a thunderstorm or other calamity.) Next, they removed the stomach.

Variations on the basic format of this first salmon ceremony appeared up and down the coast. The Kwakiutl of Vancouver Island's east coast operated at least three. Individual fishermen performed one type when they caught their first (sockeye) salmon. Having landed the fish in his canoe, Boas explained, he pulls out the spear and prays to it.

> We have come to meet alive, Swimmer. Do not feel wrong about what I have done to you, friend Swimmer, for that is the reason why you come that I may spear you, that I may eat you, Supernatural One, you, Long-Life-Giver, you, Swimmer. Now protect us, (me) and my wife, that we may keep well, that nothing may be difficult for us, that we wish to get from you, Rich-Maker-Woman. Now call after you your father and your mother and uncles and aunts and elder brothers and sisters to come to me also, you, Swimmers.[10]

In one of the Kwakiutl collective ceremonies, the wife of the fisherman who catches the first salmon goes to the beach where she prays to it and cuts up the fish so that only the head and tail remain on the backbone. Then she roasts the carcass and carries it into the house for the guest of honour, who eats the eyes. If the roasted eyes are not eaten, salmon will vanish from the ocean. Everything possible is done to curry favour. After the flesh has been eaten too, she gathers the bones and skin, wraps them up and tosses the bundle into the sea so that new life can be rekindled and the fish return to its underwater house for another year. The final first salmon ceremony at Celilo Village prior to the completion of the Dalles Dam (20 April 1956) was a poignant and tearful occasion, presided over by the Wyams tribal chief. The occasional ceremony was held at the relocated village, with fish caught elsewhere but, largely stripped of meaning, they soon fizzled out completely.[11]

Not every salmon-eating people performed a formal ceremony. Yet its absence does not preclude a reverential attitude or salmon 'myth' (Gunther's term). One story tells of a boy who arrives in salmon territory and is instructed to slay some children for food but to toss the saved bones into the sea so the children will come back to life. He then goes home bearing plenty of fish. Various taboos governed tribal lives. The Kwakiutl maintained that twins of the same sex were previously salmon and

The Maidu tribe of northwest California revived its first salmon ceremony in 1995. Next to the fish in this picture (taken at the ceremony held in September 2001 at the Feather River, Oroville) is a small foil package containing its diced-up fins that will be thrown onto the fire as an offering.

that their fathers therefore had special duties of propitiation. Others regarded the birth of twins during salmon season as an ill omen and prevented the parents from fishing or eating salmon. When Euro-Americans moved into salmon country, native peoples blamed the disappearance of salmon from their rivers on non-compliance with their taboos regarding twins.[12]

Asian salmon peoples also held first fish ceremonies (*asir chep nomi* in the Ainu language). The Ainu's various animal gods disguise themselves as humans and lead similar lives. They watch over people and, assuming animal form, travel to the human world to bring food. Ainu ceremonies expressing gratitude to their salmon god, *kamuy-chep* (which translates as 'fish that goes to the place of the deities'),[13] were even more complicated than their North American counterparts. The salmon spirits who came bearing salmon were divided into particular groups, each with its own leader (headman). Prayers and offerings of sacred shaved willow sticks (*inaw*) were given at the local headman's house to the fire-spirit (*apehuchi kamuy*), who has special powers of vision, and the river-owning spirit (*pet-torun kamuy*). Having been properly entertained, each salmon spirit re-assumes human form and returns to its watery home. The fire spirit reports back to the river spirit on how the Ainu treated the salmon spirits. The river spirit then files a final report with the grand *kamuy*, who decides whether to send the salmon back the following year.

For killing salmon, the Ainu used a ceremonial club of a white wood such as willow. The first salmon was passed into the first fisher's house through a 'god window' reserved for this purpose. The rest of his settlement group were invited to partake of his first catch. Offerings of rice and malt (for brewing sake) were wrapped in bamboo leaf and placed next to the first fish's head. This first salmon, offered to the resident fire spirit, had to be cut with the same knife used for carving *inaw*. Another ceremony marked the end of the fishing season.[14] These rituals were observed well into the twentieth century as the Ainu fished in defiance of laws enacted in the 1880s to reserve salmon exclusively for commercial fisherman operating at sea.[15]

The Ulchi, the native peoples of the northern Amur River region in Siberia, and the Nyvkh (Gilyak) of the lower Amur River and Sakhalin Island, also held first salmon ceremonies. Twice a year, to greet the spring and autumn runs, the Ulchi stuck two sacred sticks carved from riverbank willow into the river bottom near the bank about a foot apart and launched, between them, a little birch bark boat filled with food offerings – including salmon. Meanwhile, they entreaty Temu, their god of rivers, oceans and lakes (an old man who lives underwater), to send salmon, though they are careful not to sound greedy, requesting only small fish.[16] Georg Wilhelm Steller reported that observance of a first fish ceremony by the rejoicing Kamtschadales of Kamchatka greatly annoyed their Russian overlords for whom they fished, 'for however impatient the master may be to taste the new fish, the fishermen will have the first, looking upon it as a great sin if they do not eat it themselves, and with all due ceremonies'.[17]

The pre-Christian world of nature in the British Isles was no less animated and enchanted than the aboriginal domains of the north Pacific. Animals were powerful spiritual beings that connected people to the Celtic other world by crossing blurred and porous boundaries. Those most adept at navigating between these two realms were the bards and seers who could inhabit the skins of other creatures. Taliesin, the revered sixth-century Welsh bard and seer, acquired the wisdom of the other-than-human life forms through a shape-shifting sequence that changed him into a hare, a salmon, a bird and, finally, a grain of wheat, each form representing one of the four elements: earth, water, air and fire. In a collection of tenth- and eleventh-century Welsh tales based on early mythology (first preserved in the Peniarth manuscripts, *The Mabinogion*, *c*. 1225), the Salmon of Llyn Llyw stars as the world's oldest and wisest animal, which King Arthur must find to set free Mabon ap Modron, the Welsh god of music, love and fertility. For only the salmon knows where he is imprisoned. Mabon's liberators ride the salmon into Gloucester prison and release him.

Celtic mythology associates salmon with knowledge, prophecy and inspiration because of the fish's uncanny ability to return to its birthplace. The most famous role for the salmon of knowledge (*Breadan Feasa*) is in the legend of Finn MacCool, the most renowned of Ireland's early semi-mythical heroes, a peerless warrior, poet and seer of the third century. Before his birth, Finn's father, a Fianna chieftain, dies in battle with a rival clan leader (Goll Mac Morna). Fearing for his life, Finn's mother entrusts her newborn son to the care of a druidess and a female warrior, who raise him in secret. Spurned by kings loath to enrage Goll, Finn roams Ireland, eventually settling down (under the name of Deimne) to study with an old Druid poet and seer, Finegas the Bard. Finegas lives near the Well of Nechtan, a sacred pool of wisdom at the source of the River Boyne, because, believing himself to be the chosen one, he wants to catch its resident Salmon of Knowledge. After Finn has studied under him for a number of years, Finegas finally catches the fish (which has gained its knowledge by eating the 'nuts of wisdom' that have fallen from the sacred hazel tree that overhangs the well; the number of spots on a salmon's back were thought to indicate how many nuts it had consumed).

Finegas instructs his pupil to cook the salmon, warning Finn not to partake of it himself. While Finn is turning the roasting fish on a spit, he burns his thumb by bursting a blister that rises up on the salmon's skin and puts it in his mouth (in other versions of the story, some grease splashes onto his thumb and he licks it). On being served the fish, Finegas asks 'Did you eat of the flesh?' When Finn tells his master that he sucked his thumb after inadvertently touching the fish, Finegas recognizes him as the truly chosen one (worthy of the name Finn MacCool) and offers him the whole fish, from which he gains the salmon's knowledge.[18] Henceforth, when Finn sucks his thumb, he can prophesy the future. He then avenges his father's death and kills Goll.

Salmon taboos also governed the activities of early Britons. One particular custom from the Outer Hebridean island of Lewis was recounted in Boethius' acclaimed *History of Scotland* (1527). Martin Martin, a Gaelic-speaking native of Skye who was a geographer and map maker, repeated this story (as prime evidence of the remnants of a backward and superstitious pagan culture that hung on where Protestantism had not yet shone its modernizing light), after a visit in the 1690s: 'The natives in the village of Barvas retain an ancient custom of sending a man very early to cross Barvas River, every first day of May, to prevent any female crossing it first; for that would hinder the salmon from coming into the river all the year round.'[19]

PICTURING SALMON

Pictorial representations complement these performative expressions of salmon significance. The first European salmon art, from 16,000–9,000 BC, was found in the caves of Altamira in northern Spain. First explored in the 1870s, Altamira is best known for its ceiling painting of 15 large bison. The pre-literate Magdalenians also depicted wild boar, horses and deer. But various artefacts have also been located here. Among the axes and

At Gorge d'Enfer, Périgord, France, an overhang features an extremely rare sculpture of a salmon (probably life-size at a metre long) that has given the rock shelter its name of Abri du Poisson. Between 34,000 and 12,000 years old, it was discovered in 1912, when (as is clearly visible) collectors from the Berlin Museum of Anthropology tried unsuccessfully to cut it out.

arrow heads perfectly protected from the erosive forces of wind and water in Atlamira's deepest recesses was a piece of reindeer antler etched with a salmon motif, evidently part of a harpoon for spearing salmon running up the river Pas that flows below the cave.

If, though, as seems likely, the main quarry of these late Palaeolithic Pyreneans became salmon once they had hunted out large mammals, why have so few sculpted representations been located? (The best known is the metre-long – probably life-size – image of the fish on the overhang of Abri du Poisson cave in southwest France's Gorge d'Enfer). Salmon probably feature infrequently because they were so common. Cave art usually depicted the most feared and highly prized of animals; just because the Magdalenians covered their cave ceilings with bison does not mean they actually killed a lot. This also holds for the pre-written cultures of North American tribes. Comparatively few salmon feature on the northwest coast's totem poles (orca, raven, eagle and bear abound on these carved and painted assemblages of symbols and images that were arranged to tell a story by being 'read' from bottom to top). Salmon appear more frequently in recent and contemporary designs but this is more a reflection of the perceptions and expectations of non-Native patrons. As in prehistoric Europe, salmon were probably too everyday to be routinely elevated to art form.

Over in Scotland, one of the most striking Pictish symbol stones from the early medieval era (c. AD 750–900) depicts fish that are almost certainly salmon. The 1.6-metre-long block of sandstone was struck by a plough just a foot below the surface of a field at Inchyra House, near Perth, in 1945. The Inchyra slab's most recent use had been as the cover-stone of a grave, but judging from its shape and the orientation of the fish, its original purpose had obviously been to stand upright.[20]

A more obvious and recent, if easily overlooked, source of visual information about salmon is the imagery stuck to salmon tins. Early twentieth-century British Columbian brand names ('Reigning', 'Royal Line', 'Coronet', 'Duke' and 'Empress') underscored the prestigious reputation of the king of fish

A Pictish symbol stone of AD 500–700, which bears a fish (most likely a salmon) on both sides, unearthed during the ploughing of parkland near Perth in 1945.

Tinned salmon label: 'Indian Brand', Victoria, BC.

Tinned salmon label: 'Walrus Brand'.

John West tinned salmon label: 'Riverside Pasture' brand.

through association with royalty, particularly in view of the primacy of both British and overseas imperial markets. Archtypical Canadian motifs such as beaver, maple leaf and Mountie were another potent marketing strategy.[21] Other labels simply carried pictures of creatures associated with far northern regions. Native peoples, when they featured, were caricatures of the Plains Indian 'brave' with his generic moccasins and feathered war bonnet. Popular Euro-American stereotypes cropped up again in a far-fetched colour advertisement for John West

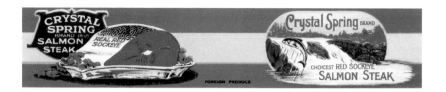

salmon that appeared in a British magazine in 1929: a cowboy and a (Plains) Indian – both of them a long way from cattle country – canoe together down a river fringed by thick, towering trees. The west coast peoples whose lives the fish defined rarely featured.

Tinned salmon label: John West, 'Crystal Spring' brand.

The labels of the premier British brand, John West, originally concentrated on John West himself or fishermen. 1930s advertisements featured men whose jobs were physically demanding and, presumably, were in particular need of salmon's unrivalled sustenance: scaffolders, firemen and coal miners. John West adopted its famous slogan, 'Insist on the Best', during this decade, and 'the best' Pacific coho, the firm insisted, was equal in quality, flavour and colour to the finest 'British river caught salmon' (labels showed aristocratic-looking anglers clad in

The Disney polar bear advertising 'Gold Seal' canned salmon.

Cover of an issue of the *Pacific Rescue* cartoon strip, c. 1950, a story based on a Canfisco fishing boat's rescue of crewmen of a us bomber that crashed off the coast of British Columbia in February 1950.

159

Edouard Manet, *Still-life with Salmon*, 1864–5, oil on canvas.

tweeds and waders, holding their rods and displaying their catch in a bucolic riverbank setting). During World War II, British troops marched and fought with Pacific salmon in their stomachs. Between 1942 and 1946, 80 per cent of British Columbia's canned salmon pack was destined for British troops and Britain's civilian front. Though little salmon was available for domestic sale, holding the attention of Canadian consumers was considered a good investment for peacetime.[22] So the Disney Corporation created a group of cartoon characters, notably Wally the Walrus, Sylvester the Bear, Sammy the Salmon and an unnamed polar bear to advertise the Canadian Fishing Company's (Canfisco) new top brand of 'fancy' sockeye, 'Gold Seal'.

The look of the fish itself has shifted as well as the associated imagery. Whole salmon sometimes appeared in the early days, if rarely in their natural context – an exceptional label ('Crystal

160

Spring', see page 159) shows the salmon engaged in its quintessential activity of leaping up falls. Between the 1930s and 1950s, labels were particularly graphic; hunks of raw fish – sometimes including the tail – sat in pools of what looks like blood but which was identified as 'rich red oil'. Some labels (recalling Manet's *Still-life with Salmon*) specified 'Middle Cut', depicting a fish halved to display the succulent centre. Some sections of fish had their skin partly peeled back, their flesh almost impossibly red. In the 1970s, photographs replaced artwork and labels became increasingly minimalist to focus attention on the product itself. They show a sanitized chunk of rosy fish garnished with a sprig of parsley and some sliced lemon or cucumber.

LITERARY SALMON

'Rosy red' flesh was a quality also celebrated in the fourth-century poem in which the fish makes its literary debut: Decimus Magnus Ausonius's paean to the River Moselle:

> Nor would I leave thee unsung, thou rosy red
> Salmon, whose broad tail from the middle depth
> Ripples the surface, when thy hidden course
> Betrays its motion. Though, with scaly coat
> Of mail, tho' smooth in front, art doomed to grace
> Some noble banquet . . . Upon thy head
> How notable the markings, while to the stream
> Thy belly swings, swollen with coils of fat![23]

Leaping forward – and northwestward – to early twentieth-century Ireland, salmon sport in various poems of W. B. Yeats, an avid fisherman whose family owned a flour mill next to the salmon-weir at the falls on the Ballisodare River, County Mayo. In 'Sailing to Byzantium' (1926), salmon stand for irrepressible fecundity and the sheer exuberance of physical existence.

> That is no country for old men. The young
> In one another's arms, birds in the trees
> – Those dying generations – at their song,
> The salmon-falls, the mackerel-crowded seas,
> Fish, flesh, or fowl, commend all summer long
> Whatever is begotten, born, and dies.
> Caught in that sensual music all neglect
> Monuments of unaging intellect.

Fellow Irish poet Seamus Heaney is just as keen to relate a fundamental salmon characteristic to the human condition. A short early poem, 'The Salmon Fisher to the Salmon' (1969), dwells on the primordial urge to return:

> your exile in the sea
> Unconditionally cancelled by the pull
> Of your home water's gravity

Heaney evokes a fleeting but deep relationship between the angler and his quarry. Standing in mid-river and casting his fly, currents eddying around him, the fisherman feels at one with the object of his desire in a shared watery medium ('I go, like you, by gleam and drag'). Then he catches the fish and shatters the illusion of kinship. He recognizes his responsibility for the salmon's homecoming 'grief' and makes his own journey home, bearing the marks of his culpability (which are also the vestiges of his former salmon self).

We're both annihilated on the fly.
You can't resist a gullet full of steel.
I will turn home fish-smelling, scaly.[24]

A salmon-inspired poet in North America is Tim Bowling, who has worked as a deckhand on a Fraser River gill-netter. Many poems in his first collection, *Low Water Slack*, pivot on the fish he sees as regal, heraldic and holy, dignified until the bittersweet end. In 'Sockeye Salmon', Bowling compares its silver scales to the 'breastplate of Kings' and describes eyes that 'never stop believing in the holy purpose of the flesh: they know their dying is divine'. The bodily conversion prior to spawning reminds him of the vivid colours of a court jester as they 'make the abdicating leap . . . from instruments of god to capering fools'.[25]

Bowling's salmon poems are deeply empathetic and visceral. But Sherman Alexie, a Coeur d'Alene/Spokane Indian from eastern Washington, demonstrates a more atavistic and intimate, if less overtly emotional link with the fish. In the title poem, 'The Man Who Loves Salmon', of a recent collection of salmon poetry, the hen salmon is the man's lover and her offspring are his 'finned children'. 'Creation Story' evokes the profound dependency of Alexie's tribe:

I catch the salmon
with my bare hands
and offer it
to my mother

she opens the fish
and finds
a city of Indians
living among the thin bones[26]

Europe's salmon poet par excellence is Ted Hughes. In 1961, Hughes moved to North Tawton in north Devon, a small town near the Taw, a salmon stream that rises on Dartmoor and empties into the Bristol Channel. *River*, a collection published in 1983, the year before he became poet laureate, contains his greatest clutch of salmon poems. 'The Morning Before Christmas' features dead males in their 'wedding finery' trapped in a sluice at a weir. In 'New Year', Hughes captures the perfect balance between life and death, the symbiosis between 'the lank, dying fish' and 'the ticking egg' at the redds that are both marriage bed and graveyard (and characterized in 'October Salmon' as the 'only mother he ever had'). 'An August Salmon' mulls over the unflinching demise of a fish 'mortally wounded by love and destiny'.

> His beauty bleeding invisibly
> From every lift of his gills

Ever since Aesop's Fables, animals have been infused with symbolic value and associated with human qualities within the exemplary 'book of nature'. The crab, for instance, because of its sideways mode of locomotion, has been a by-word for inconstancy. But the salmon has traditionally been seen as an unambiguous creature, representing only nobility. In 'September Salmon', the selflessness that serves the next generation captivates Hughes, and 'October Salmon' demonstrates just how easily salmon are personified.

> Death has already dressed him
> In her clownish regimentals, her badges and decorations,
> Mapping the completion of his service,
> His face a ghoul-mask, a dinosaur of senility, and his
> whole body

A fungoid anemone of canker –

What a change! From that covenant of Polar Light
To this shroud in the gutter!
What a death-in-life – to be his own spectre!
His living body become death's puppet,
Dolled by death in her cruel paints and drapes

At the final reckoning, the salmon's emblematic quality is grace under pressure:

The epic poise
That holds him so steady in his wounds, so loyal to his
    doom, so patient
In the machinery of heaven[27]

Hughes was another ardent angler among authors. His last interview, appropriately, appeared in an American fishing magazine.[28] He was active in the Westcountry Rivers Trust and supported the work of the Atlantic Salmon Trust, which published (1985) a limited edition of 156 hand-set, numbered and signed copies of his most acclaimed salmon poem, 'October Salmon'.

An earlier, more gung-ho salmon fisherman among British writers was Charles Kingsley. Having recently finished his classic children's fantasy tale, *The Water-Babies*, he spent his 1862 summer vacation salmon fishing in Scotland. After fishing the Tay, he travelled west to the Duke of Argyll's castle at Inveraray, where the River Aray, he told his mother, held more salmon than water.[29] As well as dramatizing the plight of the notorious 'climbing boys', *Water-Babies* reflects on the salmon's wretched condition (though it was much more successful in exposing the young sweep's predicament and galvanizing action to improve his lot).

Water-Babies also yields insights into the Victorian salmon's social status. Tom, the hapless and grimy apprentice sweep on the run, leaps into a stream's crystal waters to cleanse himself and floats downstream. On reaching the estuary (having drowned and changed into a tiny elf-like creature), he encounters an impressive fish heading upriver, ten times bigger than a large trout and a hundred times his own size: 'Such a fish!', marvels the over-awed water-baby, 'shining silver from head to tail, and here and there a crimson dot; with a grand hooked nose and grand curling lip, and a grand bright eye, looking round him as proudly as a king, and surveying the water right and left as if all belonged to him. Surely he must be the salmon, the king of all the fish.' The fierce otter that Tom had previously encountered reinforces this persona, portraying the salmon as a haughty fellow with a low opinion of other fish ('they are so proud and bully the little trout, and the minnows').

The salmon, however, assures Tom that he has nothing to fear because salmon are all 'true gentlemen'. The biggest salmon is also the model Victorian husband, escorting his

Paddling down to the ocean, the former chimney-sweep's apprentice in Charles Kingsley's *Water-Babies* (1863) is dwarfed alongside a magnificent salmon steaming in the opposite direction.

mate, fussing over her and urging her to rest, unlike the 'vulgar' chub, roach and pike that 'have no high feelings, and take no care of their wives'. Trout, the salmon pair explain, are 'relations of ours who do us no credit'. Instead of doing the manly thing and heading off to sea, they hang around, eating anything they can grab, so impudent and depraved they even eat young salmon and force themselves on lady salmon. If a trout were to commit the ultimate act of transgression and try to mate with a female salmon, the male salmon warns, he would have to kill them both.[30]

A more accurate account of salmon behaviour was communicated by Henry Williamson. Ironically, the finest salmon novel in English was the work of an author best known for dramatizing the life of an animal that introduces itself to Tom in *Water-Babies* as the lord of the salmon: the otter. Henry Williamson's *Salar the Salmon* (1935) was set in the same territory as *Tarka the Otter* (1927) – north Devon. Williamson wrote *Salar* in his late thirties while residing at Shallowford House, Filleigh. He enjoyed fishing rights on the River Bray, which ran through the deer park. Just a stone's throw from his house was 'Humpy Bridge', where he fished for trout and salmon in Bridge Pool.

Henry Williamson poses with his 9-pound salmon caught in the River Bray at Shallowford, Devon, April 1935.

Though it failed to match the success of *Tarka*, *Salar* again demonstrated Williamson's talent for crawling inside another creature's skin to craft an endearing animal personality. Salar is a five-year-old, 9-kilogram cock salmon on his spring run, an immensely powerful fish, his shoulders 'hog-curved with stored power' for the spawning run that drives the narrative forward. Quitting the Atlantic, Salar enters the 'Severn Sea' (Bristol Channel) and swims into the estuary of the 'Two Rivers' (Taw and Torridge). Next, he heads up the Taw, turning north again where the Mole joins, and northwest at the Mole's junction with the Bray. En route to his spawning grounds on Exmoor's southern

This monogram by the renowned animal artist Charles F. Tunnicliffe features on the final page of the first edition of Henry Williamson's *Salar the Salmon* (1935).

Tunnicliffe's picture of a spawning at the redds on Exmoor appeared in the first illustrated edition (1936) of *Salar the Salmon*.

slopes, Salar passes right under Williamson's nose at Humpy Bridge.

Williamson was well versed in Salar's natural history by reading back issues of *Salmon and Trout* magazine. He knew that scale rings revealed Salar's story and noted his outward changes in colour prior to spawning. Grotesque fungus spreads across his head and with his hooked jaws he can no longer close his mouth properly.[31] 'In slow pulse after slow pulse', Williamson reflects on Salar's post-spawning condition, 'his life's sweetness had been drawn from him, leaving with each emptiness a greater inflaming desire, which during the day lapped about the wasted body with dreams of an everlasting sea of rest.'[32] Salar pulsates with blood, emotion, instinct, sensuality and wildness, his return journey exhibiting the 'everlasting action' of 'racial immortality'. Williamson's reputation has been tarnished in the public mind by his sympathy for fascist ideals and admiration for Hitler's pre-war Germany (he joined Sir Oswald Mosley's British Union of Fascists in 1937 and was briefly imprisoned under the Defence of the Realm Act when war broke out). Given that Williamson found the aesthetic dimensions of the fascist worldview enormously appealing, is Salar a Nietzschean super-fish, the embodiment of primordial heroism and every other romantic quality of intellectual fascism?

The salmon as human allegory also suffuses Scottish author Neil Gunn's stream-of-consciousness story about going home, *Highland River* (1937). After the traumatic experience of youthful service in World War I, the novel's main protagonist, Kenn, eventually returns to his childhood village. His parents and brother are now dead and 'strangers' occupy his old home. His struggle as a nine-year-old against a huge salmon trapped in a pool supplies the novel's frenzied opening scene. The 14-kilogram fish – as long as Kenn is tall – is more or less a match in

Alex Main's bronze sculpture at the harbour in Dunbeath, Caithness, Scotland, was inspired by a dramatic incident in Neil Gunn's novel *Highland River* (1937), in which a boy poaches a salmon almost as big as himself in the Dunbeath river and hauls it off on his back. It was erected in 1991 to mark the centenary of Gunn's birth in the village.

physical strength. But he kills it with stones and his bare hands.

Kenn's Highland river represents sanity and purity in a crazy, contaminated world. 'Our river took a wrong turning somewhere!' he laments, but adds that 'we haven't forgotten the source'. Impelled by an 'impulsive need' to get back to the source of life and of himself, he makes for the headwaters of his childhood river (a place he has never been before). Moving up beyond familiar territory, he passes tiny spawning pools, feeling sympathy for the salmon as their 'strength was spent magnificently, utterly, almost to the point of death' and, for the first time, feels somewhat ashamed of his primordial urge to kill them. He, too, feels at home here, because he, too, has almost consummated his journey: 'He was drawing back into his own. He could feel the pull – as the salmon felt it.'[33]

The ideas of the Swiss psychiatrist Carl Gustav Jung also shaped a highly influential non-fiction work – Joseph Campbell's *The Hero with a Thousand Faces* (1949). Campbell identifies a 'monomyth' that conforms to an ageless format regardless of time and place: the hero leaves his familiar world to embark on a quest and, after a long journey beset by trials and tribulations that involves the irrevocable crossing of watersheds, he finally returns home. Regardless of how effectively this formula encapsulates the essence of mythology, Boria Sax reflects, it 'clearly describes the lives of salmon'.

> They leave their homes to travel downstream . . . to the sea . . . Near the conclusion of their lives, they return upstream to their place of their birth to spawn. If the theory of Campbell is even partially correct . . . it helps explain the fascination of salmon. The life cycle of the salmon presents an archetypal image of the heroic quest. Certainly, the accomplishment of the salmon in swimming upstream is a feat of heroic proportions. Their magnificent leaps also suggest transcendence.[34]

Perhaps the salmon is the most ancient of all western heroes and maybe its incredible journey across the thresholds of salt and freshwater is the original quest that inspired the first human stories of heroes and their odysseys.

SCULPTED SALMON

For all their epic attributes, wild salmon would require supernatural powers to transcend all the obstacles that we have tossed

Cast by Pete Langley, owner of the Port Townsend Foundry in Washington state, 'Ali the Aluminum Salmon' weighs 400 pounds. Most of the other fish in the 'Soul Salmon' project are fibreglass.

across their path. Contemporary sculptures of salmon in public spaces in Oregon and Washington represent an effort to raise public consciousness of native salmon, and money for their conservation. Tom Jay and Sara Mall Johani, who live on Washington's northern Olympic Peninsula, spearhead this crusade. A former salmon fisherman and bronze foundry operator turned sculptor, Jay is helping to restore the summer run of chum to his local river, Chimacum Creek. 'Heroic Chum', a two-metre bronze head thrusting out of the tarmac in a strip mall parking lot on the fringes of Port Townsend, conveys the hope that the beleaguered fish will return. His most renowned sculpture, though, is 'Fin', a fibreglass 7.5-metre, 580-kilogram female chum that travels to schools and fairs to promote the conservation work of Wild Olympic Salmon (founded in 1987). Fin's inside walls depict stream bank life and a stream flows through her from tail to mouth. Johani's creations include orange glass beads in the form of salmon eggs, each with a tiny black dot in the middle to represent the developing eye in a month-old egg sac, and a 'salmorang' inscribed with the slogan 'Salmon Come Back.'[35]

Canned Salmon created by Vladimir Shakov and Chris Wooten as part of the 'Soul Salmon' project (2001) is made from recycled cans.

Johani is president of Soul Salmon 2001, a public art project that installs 'artful' salmon around Puget Sound. 'Imagine coming to work one day and being startled by an eight foot salmon you would meet only in a dream', explains the project's website. 'It might be wearing a hat, sporting flames or sprouting trees or cloaked in poems praising rivers. Imagine the effects of hundreds of such salmon throughout the state!' Sponsored by businesses, charities and civic bodies, local artists are decorating hundreds of 2.4-metre fibreglass salmon. Soul Salmon's initial venture, 'Soul Salmon, The First Splash', displayed 35 sculptures between November 2001 and April 2002 (displays of salmon sculpture have since spread to other parts of the west coast). One of them, Ela Brickson's 'Save the Last Dance for Me', gave irrevocable fate a humorous slant. 'Esmeralda', dressed to kill for her last fling, sports a party frock and her tail splays into legs clad in striped knee socks. In her pink high heels, she cavorts on a plinth of gravel. 'If it was me going to my last resting place', Brickson explains, 'I would dress up, put on my high heels and have a great time.'[36] The purpose of Esmeralda and her kin is to 'reintroduce and revitalize wild salmon in our imagination and experience as a totem of local culture and keystone of northwest ecosystems . . . reaffirming the old notion that community is grounded in the commons that salmon embody'.[37]

SALMON ARE US

Soul Salmon's 'salmon commons' is an arresting metaphor for a physical space that people and other creatures occupy communally, a shared home where land, waters and natural resources are used for common good. This salmon commons has even been elevated to nation status. You will search conventional maps of North America in vain for Salmon Nation. For some though, it is very real. Inspired by the title of a book by Jim Lichatowich and Seth Zuckerman (*Salmon Nation: People, Fish, and our Common Home*, 1999), this new country is a transnational entity whose terrestrial domain is defined by the realm of its iconic animal, stretching down the Pacific Coast from Alaska to northern California. The brainchild of Ecotrust (Portland, Oregon), which published the aforementioned book, Salmon Nation was born in 2003. Landward boundaries are defined by the outer edges of the watersheds within which Pacific species have spawned historically. Salmon Nation's underlying objective (a tall order) is to promote a sense of place among all its human residents through a bioregional notion of belonging that transcends the usual divisions of race, ethnicity, class, gender and religion. An emerging Declaration of Salmon Nation based on citizen input currently includes the following uplifting clauses:

Whereas: the rains fall in Salmon Nation, the forests grow in Salmon Nation, the hills and mountains of Salmon Nation constrict flowing rivers into cascading streams, and the Salmon return throughout Salmon Nation, notwithstanding the efforts of the human citizens of Salmon Nation. Therefore: let the rains fall, let the forests grow, let the streams flow, let the salmon swim, so that all the citizens of Salmon Nation may be fed. Whereas: The spirit and blood of First Nation Peoples and Salmon have fertilized the rainforests of home and spawned the Salmon Nation and whereas First Nations have been joined recently in this eternal responsibility by non-first nations citizens. Therefore: all who now call these Rainforests of Salmon Nation home, share in the responsibility for its protection given to us by the creator.

Whereas: the sight of salmon leaping elevates the spirit. Therefore: we love them.[38]

Festivals that revolve around the fish's annual return express that love. Tokens of profound affection and esteem are evident in East Asia too. The first accomplishment of the Come Back Salmon Society (founded in 1979) was to establish a Living Museum of Toyohira Salmon in Sapporo (Hokkaido's capital).[39] A two-day Ainu first fish celebration was reinstated in Sapporo in the early 1990s.[40] In September 2004, the second Sakhalin Salmon Festival on the Kamchatka Peninsula brought together those working to protect wild salmon around the Pacific. The 'Declaration of Salmon Rights', which all delegates signed, proclaimed that 'Salmon has the right to live. Salmon has the right to pure water. Salmon has the right to reproduce'.

In its effort to exercise that right to reproduce, the salmon struggles upstream. This contra flow, Sax believes, is what we find particularly captivating. 'All of what we call "civilization"', he speculates, 'is perhaps, a sort of swimming "against the current" of the natural world. Perhaps the human identification with salmon may be . . . that both seem to contradict natural patterns.'[41] So salmon are us. Yet this sense of kinship does not prevent us from eating salmon – as a close relationship with dogs, cats and horses prevents most North Americans and Europeans from eating these best friends. On the contrary, consuming salmon flesh is an act of communion and thanksgiving for those of us who dwell in salmon nations. Their flesh becomes our bodies. The next step is for us to become what Soul Salmon calls 'salmon people'. Salmon are us and we are salmon.

Conclusion: Salmon Past, Present and Future

The literary expressions of appreciation and affection for the salmon and the other cultural recordings of salmon significance registered in the previous chapter are all predicated on the perennial attributes of the wild salmon. When writing about what it means to be a salmon and what the salmon means to us, Williamson, Hughes and Alexie had an unequivocal idea of what made a salmon a salmon. Yet we can no longer speak of a singular salmon with an unchanging identity. Whether we like it or not, there are now many kinds of salmon: wild, hatchery, farmed and transgenic. And we have had a hand in making them all – the essential, wild one that the poets, novelists and storytellers have enshrined being arguably the most heavily constructed of them all. The product of history and human intervention (cultural as well as ecological) is a fish with multiple identities whose differences sometimes go far beyond those that distinguish the various wild species of the Pacific and Atlantic. The George W. Bush administration is seeking to define hatchery raised fish as biologically equivalent to wild ones for the purpose of counting salmon. Yet as a Canadian scientist has stressed, artificially propagated salmon are smaller and less genetically diverse than their wild counterparts: 'It's like saying Chihuahuas and wolves are the same'.[1]

Rather than leave the salmon as a woeful shadow of its former splendid self, it's far more satisfying to serve it up as a creature that is both natural and mechanical, a self-willed biotic entity and a product of our ingenuity. The plurality of the salmon has given rise to some (not so) delicious ironies. During a recent visit to northern California, at the height of the California King salmon season, the salmon on the barbecue grill had come all the way from a Norwegian farm. And there's another twist in the tale: many farmed salmon are now grown in Chile, thousands of miles south of the fish's historic range. To compound the anomaly, many of Chile's stock are the Atlantic's *Salmo salar*.

What does it mean to be a salmon today? For a farmed salmon on the west coast of Scotland, being a salmon means circling around a floating cage and eating pellets containing dyes that impart the hue that its wild counterpart derives from krill. For a salmon raised in a hatchery, being a salmon may mean carrying around a tag. The coded wire tag is a tiny piece of metal injected into the head that contains information about its origins. When it returns as an adult to the river of its release, the tag is located with metal detectors and read under a microscope.[2] The 'PIT' (Passive Integrated Transponder) tag is even more sophisticated – a miniscule glass tube containing an antenna and microchip (all weighing just 0.06 gm) that is injected into a salmon's body cavity. The transponder (which gives 'fish and chips' a whole new meaning) is activated by sensors at dams that read data from fish passing within 18 cm and feed them into a computer. Each PIT tag carries a unique barcode enabling individual identification.

For a wild smolt heading down the Columbia to the Pacific, being a salmon means travelling parts of the way on barges, trucks and even planes. As they approach one of the mega-dams that block their passage, the young fish are diverted onto these 'salmon taxis' and reunited with their river below. As a Native American noted wryly in the mid 1980s: 'Wheat used to be transported on land and the fish were in the river. Now wheat is moved on the river, and young fish are transported on roads.'[3] This new form of assisted passage may strike us as the ultimate absurdity, arch-symbol of the revolutionary and deplorable changes over the past 130 years that have metamorphosed the fish we call salmon almost beyond recognition. But since humans first starting catching them, salmon have not dwelled in a world entirely of their own and on their own. And yet, despite our reshaping of the fish itself and our shaping of its world, the salmon has not been reduced to an entirely cultural creature. The irrepressible salmon returning to its former haunts in some English rivers, however tentatively, curbs the temptation to view the fish primarily as hapless victim subject to endless manipulation. Especially since these recolonizers may well be of hatchery origin (rather than 'strays'), this reoccu-pation suggests the salmon's continuing role as a protagonist that helps shape its own unpredictable story, going against the flow in more than one sense in a bid to recover a former identity.

What next for the salmon? Today's wild Atlantic population numbers an estimated 3.5 million. Pacific salmon are far more abundant at around 500 million. But even if all the dams were torn down and all the farms were shut down, the wild salmon's future would not be guaranteed. Global warming has huge implications for a fish that likes its water cold. The conse-quences of genetic engineering are also potentially enormous. What will it mean to be a salmon that grows as much in six months as a wild salmon does in six years? And will this fish be a first cousin to the wild salmon or a distant relative?

I shall pose the big question one last time. Why have we humans spent so much time thinking about the salmon and what the salmon has become? Because the salmon is the epitome of cosmopolitanism, roaming vast distances and disregarding international boundaries. Because the salmon is a connecting force across time and space. Salmon link Devon's little East Dart River with British Columbia's mighty Fraser. They connect the prehistoric Ainu with today's supermarket shopper, and the former's drying racks with the latter's microwave. At the same time, the salmon that swim through these worlds and link these lives are intensely parochial creatures, endemic to very particular places, providing a natural foundation for regional identity in a McWorld of rampant homogenization where everything threatens to taste the same.[4]

We of the northern hemisphere are entranced by the salmon because we see the best of ourselves in the wild fish – nobility, determination, selflessness, endurance and love of home. We are intrigued by salmon because we have abused them as well as depended on and revered them – rough treatment that has lent the fish a tragic air. And we are passionate about salmon, passionate because our thoughts have become just as entwined with them as our economies. Over the centuries we have captured billions with net, spear, rod and all manner of contraption. And if ever our waters become empty of salmon of any kind, the wild one will continue to captivate us. Remember, you are a salmon.

Timeline of the Salmon

c. 50 million BC	c. 50–24 million BC	c. 12 million BC	16,000–9,000 BC
A salmonid (*Eosalmo driftwoodensis*) first appears in the fossil record in Eocene sediments in British Columbia	Fossilized skulls indicate that Salmonidae's branches (genera) were already established when the landmasses of Europe, Greenland and North America were connected	A sabre-toothed salmon (*Smilodonichthys rastrosus*) appears in the fossil record. Three metres long and weighing 180 kg, this may be a direct ancestor of today's sockeye and Chinook	First evidence of human consumption of salmon in Europe, in the caves of Altamira, northern Spain

1758	1804	1840s	1860	1864
Salmo salar first described by Linnaeus	Captain William Clark becomes the first Euro-American to record seeing and eating Pacific salmon	Victoria and Albert start spending their summer vacations fishing in the Highlands	First Royal Commission appointed to investigate and report on the state of the English and Welsh salmon fisheries	First salmon cannery on North America's west coast established on the Sacramento River, California

1934	1935	1950s	1950s	1956
First dams erected on the Columbia River	Henry Williamson publishes *Salar the Salmon*	Pink salmon transplanted to Newfoundland and the Barents Sea	Arthur Hasler and his team at the University of Wisconsin-Madison conduct experiments confirming the integral role of olfactory imprinting	The final first salmon ceremony at Celilo Village on the Columbia River

c. AD 100	1086	*c.* 1150	1609	1653
Pliny the Elder names the Atlantic salmon *Salmo salar*	Domesday Book records Britain's salmon fisheries	Salmon economy emerges on the Alaska Peninsula as Aleut villages expand and are located on rivers up which spawning sockeye migrate	English explorer Henry Hudson's party, sailing up the US river that bears his name, record a fish that many believe was a salmon	Walton's *The Compleat Angler* includes an early account of tagging experiments to test the natal stream theory

1870s	*c.* 1900	1910s	1922
First salmon hatchery in North America opens on the McCloud River, northern California	Chinook salmon transplanted to New Zealand's South Island	Research indicates that reading a salmon's scales reveals its age and life experiences	Georgina Ballantine lands the biggest rod-caught salmon in British history on the River Tay

1958	1960s	1960s	2000	2001
Last reported salmon catch in the River Rhine	World's first salmon farms are established in Norway	US Peace Corps transplants the chinook and coho salmon to southern Chile	Aqua Bounty Farms (Waltham, MA) applies to the US Food and Drug Administration for a permit to commercially produce transgenic salmon	*Warnings from the Wild: The Price of Salmon*, a BBC2 TV documentary, examines the plight of salmon, farmed and wild, and the health risks of eating farmed salmon

References

INTRODUCTION

1 Izaak Walton, *The Compleat Angler* (London, 1964 [1653]), p. 113.
2 Leo Berg, *Freshwater Fishes of the USSR and Adjacent Countries* (Jerusalem, 1962 [1948]), p. 194.
3 Robert Hamilton, *The Natural History of British Fishes*, 2 vols (Edinburgh, 1843), vol. 2, p. 118.
4 Online at http://www.cheltenham.gov.uk/libraries/templates/options.asp?URN=1640&FolderID=0.
5 Douglas Adams, *The Salmon of Doubt: Hitchhiking the Galaxy One Last Time* (London, 2002).
6 George Rooper, *The Autobiography of the Late Salmo Salar: The Life, Personal Adventures and Death of a Tweed Salmon* (London, 1867), p. 15.
7 Georg Wilhelm Steller/Stepan Petrovich Krasheninnikov, *The History of Kamtschatka, and the Kurilski Islands, with the Countries Adjacent*, trans. James Grieve (Gloucester, 1764), p. 148.
8 Thomas Fuller, *The Worthies of England*, 3 vols, ed. John Freeman (London, 1952 [1662]), vol. 2, p. 69.
9 J. W. Jones, *The Salmon* (London, 1959), preface.
10 Robert Blatchford, *Merrie England* (London, 1893), p. 88.
11 Charles Phair, *Atlantic Salmon Fishing* (New York, 1937), p. 130.
12 Charles Dickens, 'Salmon', *All The Year Round: A Weekly Journal*, 20 July 1861, p. 406.
13 Walton, *Compleat Angler*, p. 113.

1 David Starr Jordan, *Salmon and Trout of the Pacific Coast* (Sacramento, CA, 1892), p. 1.

2 Francis Day, *British and Irish Salmonidae* (London, 1887), p. 1.

3 Salmonidae consist of 11 genera – a genus being a group of living organisms comprising related and morphologically similar species. Within these genera are 167 species, a species being a group of organisms capable of interbreeding. Family, genus and species are progressively smaller units of classification for animals and plants within Linnaeus' system of taxonomy (1735). Above the family stand the order, class, phylum and, finally, the kingdom.

4 Izaak Walton, *The Compleat Angler* (London, 1964 [1653]), p. 114.

5 Whether the salmon was originally a fresh or salt water fish has been as hotly debated as the question of its ocean of origin. The case for freshwater origins hinges on the invariable return there to spawn. If laid in salt water, ova would float; even if they sank to the bottom, they would die. Also, whereas entire genera and many species of Salmonidae live wholly in freshwater, there are no exclusively marine forms. According to the freshwater theory of origin – which still more or less holds sway – salmon began to migrate to the sea when freshwater conditions became unsuitable during glacial times. See V. Tchernavin, 'The Origin of Salmon: Is its Ancestry Marine or Freshwater?', *Salmon and Trout Magazine*, 95 (June 1939), pp. 120–40.

6 Pliny (C. Plinius Secundus), *Historia Naturali* (*The Ninth Book of Plinies Naturall History*), trans. Philemon Holland [1601], chapter 18.

7 Some earlier philologists contended that *Salmo* is of Celtic origin. See Alfred C. Andrews, 'Greek and Latin Terms for Salmon and Trout', *Transactions and Proceedings of the American Philological Association*, 86 (1955), p. 310.

8 Rainbow and cutthroat trout used to be classified as *Salmo* on a morphological basis, but were shifted to *Oncorhynchus* on evolutionary grounds in 1989. The bridge between salmon and the trout within *Oncorhynchus* is the steelhead, the rainbow's sea-running form.

9 *The History of Kamtschatka, and the Kurilski Islands, with the Countries Adjacent,* trans. James Grieve (Gloucester, 1764), pp. 145–9. Steller served as naturalist on Vitus Bering's expedition (1741–2) to locate an eastern passage to North America, which discovered Alaska.

10 Fumihiko Kato, 'Life Histories of Masu and Amago Salmon', in *Pacific Salmon Life Histories*, eds. C. Groot and L. Margolis (Vancouver, BC, 1991), p. 449.

11 Charles Hallock, *The Salmon Fisher* (New York, 1890), p. 49.

12 As quoted in W. Bullen, *The Irish Salmon Question Socially, Economically and Commercially Considered by a Naturalist and an Epicure* (Guildford, 1863), p. 15.

13 P. D. Malloch, *Life-History and Habits of the Salmon, Sea-Trout, Trout, and Other Freshwater Fish* (London, 1912), p. 138. At 18, Malloch opened a small taxidermy and fishing tackle shop in Perth that became Scotland's most renowned.

14 Tim Bowling, 'Hell's Gate: 1913', in *Low Water Slack* (Gibsons, BC, 1995), p. 17.

15 Walton, *Compleat Angler*, p. 114.

16 Andrew Young, *The Book of the Salmon* (London, 1850), p. 215; J. Arthur Hutton, *The Life-History of the Salmon* (Aberdeen, 1924), p. 12.

17 Thomas Pennant, *British Zoology*, 4 vols (London, 1769), vol. 3, p. 241; Michael Drayton, *Poly-olbion*, ed. J. William Hebel (Oxford, 1933), p. 112.

18 Walton, *Compleat Angler*, p. 114.

19 The kype represents a marvellous piece of recycling. As salmon can no longer grow bone in the usual way – they are not feeding so they cannot absorb phosphate and calcium – they must rely on their own existing supplies. Just as deer grow antlers, soft connective tissue is converted into bone.

20 Steller, *History of Kamtschatka*, p. 148.

21 William Jardine, *Illustrations of British Salmonidae with Descriptions by Sir William Jardine* (Edinburgh, 1839–41), Plate 7.

22 W.J.M. Menzies, *The Salmon: Its Life Story* (Edinburgh, 1925),

pp. 26–7.

23 Charles Darwin, *The Origin of Species* (London, 1859), p. 94; id., *The Descent of Man and Selection in Relation to Sex* (London, 1871), pp. 510–12.

24 J. W. Jones, *Salmon* (London, 1959), p. 7.

25 As quoted in Frank Buckland, *Manual of Salmon and Trout Hatching* (London, 1864), p. 17.

26 As quoted in Buckland, *Manual of Salmon and Trout Hatching*, p. 16.

27 From 'Piscator', *Fishing Gazette* (6 March 1886), as quoted in Day, *British and Irish Salmonidae*, pp. 81–2.

28 Kenneth Dawson, *Salmon and Trout in Moorland Streams* (London, 1928), p. 83.

29 Lewis Lloyd, *Field Sports of the North of Europe: A Narrative of Angling, Hunting and Shooting in Sweden and Norway* (London, 1885), p. 79.

30 Roderick Langmere Haig-Brown, *Return to the River: A Story of the Chinook Run* (New York, 1941), pp. 247–8.

31 Charles Hallock, *The Salmon Fisher* (New York, 1890), p. 12.

32 Walton, *Compleat Angler*, p. 113.

33 Humphry Davy, *Salmonia: or Days of Fly Fishing* (London, 1828), pp. 60–62.

34 Menzies, *The Salmon: Its Life Story*, p. 71.

35 William Landram McFarland, *Salmon of the Atlantic* (New York, 1925), p. 131.

36 Henry Charles Williamson, *Pacific Salmon Migration: Report of the Tagging Operations in 1925* (Toronto, 1927), p. 41.

37 Menzies, *The Salmon: Its Life Story*, p. 35.

38 Charles Kingsley, *The Water-Babies: A Fairy Tale for a Land-Baby* (London, 1901 [1863]), pp. 106–8.

39 Hector Boece (Hector Boethius), *Scotorum Historiae: Scotorum Regni Descriptio*, folio XII (Paris, 1527); translated by John Bellenden as *The Hystory and Croniklis of Scotland* (Edinburgh, 1540).

40 Boethius, *The Hystory and Croniklis of Scotland*, p. 25.

41 Walton, *Compleat Angler*, p. 116. How these ribbons and threads remained in place is something of a mystery.

42 David Starr Jordan, *Days of a Man*, 2 vols (Yonkers-on-Hudson, NY, 1922), vol. 1, p. 227.

43 Jordan, *Salmon and Trout of the Pacific Coast*, p. 14.

44 Lyall Watson, *Jacobson's Organ and the Remarkable Nature of Smell* (London, 2000), pp. 12–15.

45 Francis Trevelyan Buckland, *Natural History of British Fishes* (London, 1881), p. 302.

46 A. D. Hasler and W. J. Wisby, 'Discrimination of Stream Odors by Fishes and its Relation to Parent Stream Behaviour', *American Naturalist*, 85 (1951), pp. 223–38; A. D. Hasler, 'Odor Perception and Orientation in Fishes', *Journal of the Fisheries Research Board of Canada*, 11 (1954), pp. 107–29.

47 Arthur Hasler, *Underwater Guideposts: Homing of Salmon* (Madison, WI, 1966), pp. 55–6.

48 Ibid., p. 98.

49 V. C. Wynne-Edwards, *Animal Dispersion in Relation to Social Behaviour* (Edinburgh, 1962), p. 463.

2 EDIBLE SALMON

1 Ernest Dunbar Clark, *The Salmon Canning Industry* (Seattle, 1927), p. 11.

2 Alaska Packers Association, *Argo Red Salmon Cook Book: How to Eat Canned Salmon* (San Francisco, 1911), p. 6.

3 Tim Bowling, 'Desire', in *Low Water Slack* (Gibsons, BC, 1995), p. 71.

4 An Alaskan researcher estimated that nearly a third of salmon running up a typical stream were killed by bears before spawning. Richard F. Shuman, 'Bear Predations on Red Salmon Spawning Populations in the Karluk River System', *Journal of Wildlife Management*, 14/1 (1950), pp. 1–9.

5 Herbert Maschner and Katherine Reedy-Maschner, 'Letter from Alaska: Aleuts and the Sea', *Archaeology*, 58/2 (March/April 2005), pp. 63–4, 66–8, 70. These findings strengthen the Aleut case for extending their permitted fishing season.

6 Recent research questions the extent of this apocryphal super-

abundance on the Atlantic coast. Salmon in New England and Atlantic Canada were in fact outstripped by cod, shad, alewives and sturgeon (and early Euro-American observers often confused shad with salmon). Climatic conditions may not have been suitable for the salmon's spread into this region until relatively recently. Analysis of fish bones in New England's prehistoric middens has revealed virtually no traces of salmon.

7 Jefferson F. Moser, *Salmon and Salmon Fisheries of Alaska*: *Report of the Operation of the U.S. Fish Commission Steamer* Albatross *for the Year Ending June 30, 1898* (Washington, DC, 1899), pp. 12–13.

8 Jim Lichatowich, *Salmon Without Rivers: A History of the Pacific Salmon Crisis* (Washington, DC, 1999), pp. 25–33.

9 Hitoshi Watanabe, *The Ainu Ecosystem: Environment and Group Structure* (Seattle, 1973), p. 122.

10 Shiro Kayano, 'Who Owns the Salmon?', in *First Fish, First People: Salmon Tales of the North Pacific Rim*, ed. Judith Roche and Meg McHutchison (Seattle, 1998), pp. 41–2.

11 Arnold Henry Savage Landor, *Alone With the Hairy Ainu: Or, 3800 Miles on a Pack Saddle in Yezo and a Cruise to the Kurile Islands* (London, 1893), p. 64.

12 Ibid., p. 211.

13 W. B. Yeats, 'Preface' to Isabella Augusta (Lady) Gregory, *Gods and Fighting Men* (London, 1904).

14 Henry Lansdell, *Through Siberia*, vol. 2 (London 1882), pp. 221–3.

15 Marion Kite, 'The Conservation of a 19th Century Salmon Skin Coat', *12th Triennial Meeting, Lyon, 29 August-3 September 1999*, vol. 2, International Council of Museums Committee for Conservation (London, 1999), p. 692.

16 *The Journals of Lewis and Clark*, ed. Bernard De Voto (Boston, 1997), pp. 194, 246, 252–4, 258, 262.

17 Washington Irving, *Astoria or Anecdotes of an Enterprise Beyond the Rocky Mountains* (Norman, OK, 1964), p. 262.

18 Alexander Russel, *The Salmon* (Edinburgh, 1864), p. 3.

19 Gerald of Wales (Giraldus Cambrensis), *The History and Topography of Ireland* (Harmondsworth, 1982 [1185]), 37.

20 Francisco Tolensi, *Vita Thomae a Kempis* (1680), pp. 36–7. Online at http://64.233.183.104/search?q=cache:xDh8qgwoJrcJ:www.augustiniancanons.org/documents/liturgy_of_the_hours%2520II.htm+francis+van+tolen&hl=en.

21 Richard C. Hoffman, 'Frontier Foods for Late Medieval Consumers: Culture, Economy and Ecology', *Environment and History*, 7/2 (May 2001), pp. 131–67.

22 Fish with a high oil content like salmon do not kipper well. The perfect fish for drying is cod, because it has virtually no fat. In the chilly Arctic, it could be air dried without salt.

23 Daniel Defoe, *A Tour Through the Whole Island of Great Britain* (London, 1978 [1724–6]), pp. 635, 645.

24 A.R.B. Haldane, *The Great Fishmonger of the Tay: John Richardson of Perth & Pitfour* (Dundee, 1981), p. 14.

25 Defoe, *A Tour Through the Whole Island of Great Britain*, p. 667.

26 Richard Franck, *Northern Memoirs, Calculated for the Meridian of Scotland* (London, 1694), p. 112.

27 Walter Scott, *The Tale of Old Mortality* (Edinburgh, 1816), p. 61.

28 Kenneth Dawson, *Salmon and Trout in Moorland Streams* (London, 1928), p. 79.

29 No documentary evidence of these restrictions has ever been produced – though not for want of trying.

30 R. D. Hume, *Salmon of the Pacific Coast* (San Francisco, 1893), p. 10. Relatively few canneries operated on the Asian side of the Pacific.

31 Rudyard Kipling, *From Sea to Sea and Other Sketches: Letters of Travel*, 2 vols (London, 1904), vol. 2, pp. 35–6.

32 Steve Wells, 'John West: His Life and Dreams', c. 1992, courtesy of Steve Wells, John West Foods, Liverpool.

33 Hume, *Salmon of the Pacific Coast*, p. 10.

34 Kipling, *From Sea to Sea and Other Sketches*, vol. 2, pp. 26–7.

35 Evelyn Waugh, *Scoop* (London, 1937), p. 19.

36 William Yarrell, 'The Salmon', in *A History of British Fishes*, 2 vols (London, 1836), vol. 2, pp. 9–10. Online at http://home.planet.nl/~zoete004/salmon.htm.

37 Thomas Tod Stoddart, *The Angler's Companion to the Rivers and*

Lochs of Scotland (Edinburgh, 1847), p. 310.

38 Walter Scott, 'Salmonia', *Quarterly Review*, October 1828, online at
http://www.arthurwendover.com/arthurs/scott/prose10.html.

39 Mark Kurlansky, *Cod: A Biography of a Fish that Changed the World*
(London, 1999), p. 207.

40 Hannah Glasse, *The Art of Cookery Made Plain and Easy* (Edinburgh,
1781), p. 295.

41 John K. Walton, *Fish and Chips and the British Working Class,
1870–1940* (Leicester, 1992), pp. 23–4.

42 Claudia Roden, *The Book of Jewish Food: An Odyssey from
Samarkand and Vilna to the Present Day* (New York, 1996), p. 93.

43 Helen Stiles, 'Beauty is Skin from the Deep', *The Field*, October
2001, online at http://www.irishsalmonskinleather.com/news-
story04.htm; 'Fishy Fashion's Salmon Special', *Sun*, 21 November
2001.

44 Charles Dickens, 'Salmon', *All The Year Round: A Weekly Journal*,
20 July 1861, p. 405.

3 UNFORTUNATE SALMON

1 Charles Kingsley, *The Water-Babies: A Fairy Tale for a Land-Baby*
(London, 1901 [1863]), p. 117.

2 Mark Cioc, *The Rhine: An Eco-Biography, 1815–2000* (Seattle,
2002), pp. 162–5. In romantic folklore, the Lorelei was the perch
of a siren whose exquisite song lured boatmen to their deaths on
the rocks below.

3 Leonard Mascall, *Booke of Fishing with Hooke and Line* (London,
1590), pp. 45–6.

4 Anthony Netboy, *The Atlantic Salmon: A Vanishing Species?*
(London, 1968), p. 281.

5 Benjamin Martin, *Natural History of England*, 2 vols (London,
1759–63), vol. 2, p. 256.

6 Izaak Walton, *The Compleat Angler* (London, 1964 [1653]), p. 115.

7 Edward Wedlake Brayley, *The History and Antiquities of the Abbey
Church of St Peter, Westminster*, 2 vols (London, 1818), vol. 1, p. 6.

8 Charles Dickens, 'Salmon', *All The Year Round: A Weekly Journal*, 20 July 1861, p. 406.

9 Francis Day, *British and Irish Salmonidae* (London, 1887), p. 116.

10 William Yarrell, *History of British Fishes*, 2 vols (London, 1836), vol. 2, p. 30.

11 Frank Buckland, 'Salmon Caught in the Thames,' *Land and Water*, 9 (23 April 1870), p. 292.

12 Dickens, 'Salmon', p. 405.

13 J. W. Willis Bund, *Salmon Problems* (London, 1885), pp. 1–3.

14 Frank Buckland, *Natural History of British Fishes* (London, 1881), p. 288.

15 Buckland, 'Salmon Caught in the Thames', p. 292. In a subsequent note (reporting the results of his post mortem), Buckland dismissed rumours that the salmon had been brought to the Gravesend hotel as a hoax: *Land and Water*, 9 (30 April 1870), p. 311.

16 Fish can be most effectively preserved by casting – stuffing entails loss of scales and discoloration – and Buckland became a skilled practitioner. He worked in the basement of his house and buried the cast-off fish in his garden (or, if he was quick, returned them to the fishmongers who supplied him).

17 Augustus Grimble, *The Salmon Rivers of Scotland*, 4 vols (London, 1899–1900), vol. 2, pp. 212, 286.

18 Daniel B. Botkin, *Our Natural History: The Lessons of Lewis and Clark* (New York, 1995), pp. 188–9.

19 As it plunges down a spillway, water churns and produces nitrogen gas, resulting in super-saturation. In a cold, fast-flowing river, excess dissolved nitrogen is released into the air and oxygen levels are high, whereas the slack, warm tail waters behind dams concentrate nitrogen.

20 Joseph E. Taylor III, 'El Niño and Vanishing Salmon: Culture, Nature, History, and the Politics of Blame', *Western Historical Quarterly*, 29 (Winter 1998), pp. 455–6.

21 As quoted in W. M. Shearer, *The Atlantic Salmon: Natural History, Exploitation and Future Management* (Oxford, 1992), p. xv.

22 Jessica Maxwell, 'Swimming with Salmon', *Natural History*, 9

(1995), p. 31.

23 Though Alaska's and British Columbia's commercial fisheries remains substantial, a glut of farmed salmon from British Columbia, Chile and Norway keeps prices down.

24 Philip Lymbery/Compassion in World Farming Trust, *In Too Deep: The Welfare of Intensively Farmed Fish* (Petersfield, Hants, 2002), pp. 3, 17.

25 Clive Gammon, 'Salmon', *Punch*, 72 (16–29 January 1999), pp. 16–17.

26 John Humphrys, *The Great Food Gamble* (London, 2001), p. 148.

27 Jane Bird and Toby Moore, 'Foodies Angle for Real Fish', *Sunday Times*, 7 June 1987. Some governmental action has ensued. In 1990, Alaska banned salmon farming from state waters to protect its vibrant commercial fishery. Norway has set up a gene bank for threatened wild stocks. Iceland and Sweden have established farm exclusion zones in certain sensitive waters. Scotland also imposed restrictions (1990) on farming along the north and east coasts to protect the best remaining wild runs. Some farms have reduced stocking densities and installed metered feeding systems to minimize waste.

28 The critique of salmon farming received unparalleled publicity in a BBC2 documentary, 'Warnings from the Wild: The Price of Salmon', produced by Jeremy Bristow and presented by Julian Pettifer (7 January 2001). Though the industry dismissed it as muckraking codswallop, Bristow's documentary received the International Wildlife Film Festival's award for 2002 in the category 'environmental issues, best conservation message' and was named best TV documentary in that year's British Environmental Media Awards.

29 'Salmon Safety Scare Spawns Fear and Paranoia among Scientists', *Sunday Herald*, 7 January 2001.

30 Frode Alfnes, Atle G. Guttormsen and Gro Steine, 'Consumers' Willingness to Pay for the Color of Salmon: A Choice Experiment with Real Economic Incentives', Discussion Paper #D-19/2004, Department of Economics and Resource Management, Agricultural University of Norway, Aas, Norway, online at http://www.nlh.no/ior/publikasjoner/diskusjonsnotat2004.19.

html. Colourants account for about 15 per cent of feed costs.

31 Ronald A. Hites et al, 'Global Assessment of Organic Contaminants in Farmed Salmon', *Science*, 303 (9 January 2004), pp. 226–9.

32 Online at http://www.albany.edu/ihe/salmonstudy/graph1.html. These recommendations are based on US Environmental Protection Agency safe eating guidelines.

33 Saturation point may soon be reached in Europe and North America in terms of suitable and/or permissible sites. With no foreseeable recovery in wild fish stocks and a rapidly expanding population in the developing world, however, salmon farming will continue to seek fresh 'blue' pastures. China may be the next watery frontier.

34 Quoted in Bruce Barcott, 'Aquaculture's Troubled Harvest', *Mother Jones* (November–December 2001), online at http://www.motherjones.com/news/feature/2001/11/aquaculture.html.

35 Alexandra Morton, 'Salmon Weren't Meant to be Farmed', *Wild Earth* (Winter 1997/8), p. 53.

36 Richard Shelton, *Longshoreman: A Life at Water's Edge* (London, 2004), p. 315.

37 Tony Reichardt, 'Will Souped Up Salmon Sink or Swim?', *Nature*, 406 (July 2000), pp. 10–12.

38 Soft flesh partly reflects chronic diarrhoea attributable to oily feed; organic feed has a maximum oil content of 28 per cent.

39 Henry Williamson, *The Henry Williamson Animal Saga* (London, 1960), p. 204.

40 G. W. Mawle and N. J. Milner, 'The Return of Salmon to Cleaner Rivers – England and Wales', in *Salmon at the Edge*, ed. Derek Mills (Oxford, 2003), pp. 186–99.

4 DISPUTED SALMON

1 Charles Elmé Francatelli, *A Plain Cookery Book for the Working Classes* (London, 1861), pp. 9, 61.

2 Robert Blatchford, *Merrie England* (London, 1893), pp. 87–8.

3 Online at
   http://eawc.evansville.edu/anthology/magnacarta.htm.

4 Edward Wedlake Brayley, *The History and Antiquities of the Abbey Church of St Peter, Westminster*, 2 vols (London, 1818), vol. 1, p. 6.

5 Lord Archibald Campbell, 'Records of Argyll', as reproduced in Augustus Grimble, *The Salmon Rivers of Scotland*, 4 vols (London, 1899–1900), vol. 4, pp. 111–16.

6 Jane Bradshaw, 'Traditional Salmon Fishing in the Severn Estuary', Master's thesis, Department of Continuing Education, University of Bristol, 1996, pp. 5–7.

7 Villages along the Severn's English side remain steeped in salmon lore. The primary school and cricket club in Oldbury, where today's main employer is a nuclear power station, both have salmon logos.

8 Rudyard Kipling, *From Sea to Sea and Other Sketches: Letters of Travel*, 2 vols (London, 1904), vol. 2, p. 28. Responding to protests from commercial netters at the Columbia's mouth, Oregon and Washington banned fish wheels in 1926 and 1934 respectively.

9 Thomas Tod Stoddart, *The Art of Angling as Practised in Scotland* (Edinburgh, 1835), p. 89; id., *An Angler's Rambles and Angling Songs*, p. 382.

10 Stoddart, *Art of Angling*, p. 383.

11 Ibid., pp. 95–6.

12 Spearing is the oldest fishing method and the spear the small-scale salmon fisherman's preferred implement since prehistoric times.

13 Other methods of poaching required less effort. In nineteenth-century Kerry, poachers emptied a small basketful of a crushed plant, Irish spurge, into rivers. This stupefied salmon for a couple of miles downstream without poisoning their flesh.

14 Walter Scott, *Guy Mannering* (Edinburgh, 1815), pp. 321–6.

15 Walter Scott, 'Davy's Salmonia', *Quarterly Review* (October 1828), in 'Miscellaneous Prose Works, Vol. 1, Part 8', online at
   http://www.arthurwendover.com/arthurs/scott/prose10.html.

16 William Scrope, *Days and Nights of Salmon Fishing in the Tweed* (London, 1843), p. 189.

17 Bill Parenteau, 'A "Very Determined Opposition to the Law": Conservation, Angling Leases, and Social Conflict in the Canadian Atlantic Salmon Fishery, 1867–1914', *Environmental History*, 9 (July 2004), pp. 441, 444.

18 Roberta Ulrich, *Empty Nets: Indians, Dams, and the Columbia River* (Corvallis, OR, 1999), p. 14.

19 Online at http://www.ccrh.org/comm/river/legal/boldt.htm.

20 Lisa Mighetto and David Ebel, *Saving the Salmon: A History of the US Army Corps of Engineers' Efforts to Protect Anadromous Fish on the Columbia and Snake Rivers* (Seattle, 1994), p. 159.

21 Following pressure for a review from white fishing interests backed by the state of Washington, the Supreme Court upheld Boldt (1979), reflecting that 'except for some desegregation cases in the south the district court has faced the most concerted official and private efforts to frustrate a decree of a federal court witnessed this century'.

5 SPORTING SALMON

1 Rudyard Kipling, *From Sea to Sea and Other Sketches: Letters of Travel*, 2 vols (London, 1904), vol. 2, p. 34.

2 Current British enthusiasts include Diana Rigg, the actress (best known for her role as Emma Peel in the 1960s TV show 'The Avengers') and Jenny Hanley, actress and TV presenter.

3 Andrew N. Herd, 'A History of Fly Fishing' (no date) online at http://www.flyfishinghistory.com.

4 Quotations from *The Booke of Haukynge, Huntyng and Fysshyng, with all Necessary Properties and Medicines that are to be Kept* (Tottell, 1561), online at http://darkwing.uoregon.edu/~rbear/berners/berners.html.

5 Walton's *The Compleat Angler* (1653) is one of the most published books in English, rivalled only by the Bible and Shakespeare's complete works.

6 Online at http://www.flyfishinghistory.com.

7 Marion Shoard, *This Land is Our Land: The Struggle for Britain's*

Countryside (London, 1987), p. 101.

8 Frederic Tolfrey, *Jones's Guide to Norway, and Salmon Fisher's Pocket Companion* (London, 1848), p. xiii. In fact, Brioude, on the River Allier in southwest France, was a mecca for French and other European salmon anglers in the late nineteenth century.

9 Charles Dickens, 'Salmon', *All The Year Round: A Weekly Journal*, 20 July 1861, p. 407.

10 Augustus Grimble, *The Salmon Rivers of Scotland*, 4 vols (London, 1899–1900), vol. 1, p. xvii.

11 Ibid., vol. 2, p. 240; Thomas Tod Stoddart, *An Angler's Rambles and Angling Songs* (Edinburgh, 1866), p. 72.

12 Prince Charles to Harold Wilson, 12 September 1969, Catalogue Reference: PREM 13/3450, The National Archives, Kew, Richmond, Surrey. Charles's concern for the future of the Atlantic salmon galvanized the Wilson administration into action and helped secure new restrictions on high seas fishing within a year. See http://www.nationalarchives.gov.uk/releases/2003/january2/charles.htm.

13 Thomas Tod Stoddart, *The Art of Angling as Practised in Scotland* (Edinburgh, 1835), pp. 41–2.

14 Humphry Davy, *Salmonia; or Days of Fly Fishing* (London, 1828), p. v.

15 Walter Scott, 'Salmonia', *Quarterly Review*, October 1828, online at http://www.arthurwendover.com/arthurs/scott/prose10.html.

16 Ibid.

17 Alexander Russel, *The Salmon* (Edinburgh, 1864), pp. 15–16.

18 Christopher Lever, *They Dined on Eland: The Story of the Acclimatisation Societies* (London, 1992), p. 108.

19 Samuel Wilson, *The California Salmon, With an Account of its Introduction into Victoria* (Melbourne, 1878), p. 15.

20 Davy, *Salmonia*, pp. 119–22.

21 Lewis Lloyd, *Field Sports of the North of Europe: A Narrative of Angling, Hunting and Shooting in Sweden and Norway* (London, 1885 [1831]), p. 16. See also, id., *Scandinavian Adventures*, 2 vols (London, 1854).

22 William Bilton, *Two Summers in Norway*, 2 vols (London, 1840), vol. 1, p. 7, vol. 2, p. 266.

23 Frederic Tolfrey, *Jones's Guide to Norway, and Salmon Fisher's Pocket*

Companion (London, 1848), p. 238. It was rumoured that the author, Frederic Tolfrey (Jones was the owner of the exclusive London fishing tackle business who hired him), had never visited Scandinavia but extracted all his information from Jones's customers.

24 Rudge (*sic*), 'More Notes from Norway', *Salmon and Trout Magazine*, 37 (October 1924), p. 252.

25 Bill Parenteau, 'A "Very Determined Opposition to the Law": Conservation, Angling Leases, and Social Conflict in the Canadian Atlantic Salmon Fishery, 1867–1914', *Environmental History*, 9 (July 2004), pp. 445, 455.

26 Bill Maree, *Fishing with the Presidents* (Mechanicsburg, PA, 1999), p. xv.

27 Online at http://www.hoover.archives.gov/exhibit/Hooverstory/galley09.html.

28 John Mundt, 'The Presidential Salmon', *Yale Anglers' Journal*, 4/1 (2004), pp. 13–18.

29 Herbert Hoover, *Fishing for Fun* (New York, 1963), pp. 79–81.

30 Maree, *Fishing with the Presidents*, p. 141.

31 I have borrowed this phrase from the title of Allison Beaumont's history of female anglers at http://www.womenanglers.us/Allison_history.html.

32 Scott, 'Salmonia'.

33 Henry Flowerdew, *The Parr and Salmon Controversy* (Manchester, 1871), p. 11.

34 The 32.2 kg, 1.35-metre salmon that Buckland cast and displayed in his museum in South Kensington was netted at Newburgh on Tay in 1872.

35 G. W. Ballantine, 'Landing of the Record Tay Salmon', pp. 121–6 [no source provided], Perth Museum and Art Gallery. The record for the North Atlantic as a whole is a 34 kg, 1.73-metre fish caught in Quebec's Restigouche River on 23 June 1990 by a retired businessman. Unlike Miss Ballantine's fish, this one was released after being photographed.

36 The largest British spring salmon, at 27 kg, was also caught by a

woman, Miss Doreen Davey, at Lower Winforton on the Wye in 1932.

37 C. Billyeald, 'Women as Anglers', *Salmon and Trout Magazine*, 93 (December 1938), p. 348.
38 Kenneth Dawson, *Salmon and Trout in Moorland Streams* (London, 1947 [1928]).
39 The prize for the first salmon (released since 2001) is a trophy and a gallon of whisky donated by the ceremony's sponsors, Dewar's (based at nearby Aberfeldy).
40 Davy, *Salmonia*, pp. 94–5.
41 Fen Montaigne, 'Everybody Loves Atlantic Salmon: Here's the Catch . . .', *National Geographic*, July 2003, p. 112.

6 CULTURAL SALMON

1 Donagh MacDonagh, 'A Poaching Song', in *A Warning to Conquerors* (1968), p. 51.
2 Thomas Tod Stoddart, *The Angler's Companion to the Rivers and Lochs of Scotland* (Edinburgh, 1847), pp. 171, 143.
3 According to legend, a lady crossing the River Clyde lost her wedding ring, and her jealous husband, suspecting that she had given it to another man, entreated St Kentigern (Glasgow's patron saint, a.k.a. Mungo) to help defend his wife's honour by finding it. St Kentigern instructed a fisherman to bring him the first salmon he caught, duly finding the ring in its mouth.
4 Thomas Moule, *The Heraldry of Fish* (London, 1842), pp. 112–32.
5 James Patrick Howley, *The Beothucks, or Red Indians: The Aboriginal Inhabitants of Newfoundland* (Cambridge, 1915), p. 331. The Beothucks (extinct since the 1820s) wrapped dried or smoked salmon in parcels of bark fastened with rootlets, which were buried with their important people to sustain them on their journey to the 'Happy Hunting Grounds'.
6 Mourning Dove (Christine Quintasket), *Coyote Tales* (1933), online at http://members.cox.net/academia/coyote.html.
7 Online at http://www.indigenouspeople.net/mountsha.htm.

8 Franz Boas, *Chinook Texts*, US Bureau of American Ethnology Bulletin, 20 (Washington, DC, 1894), pp. 102–6.

9 Erna Gunther, 'An Analysis of the First Salmon Ceremony', *American Anthropologist*, 28/4 (1926), pp. 605–17.

10 Franz Boas, *Religion of the Kwakiutl Indians*, 2 vols (New York, 1930), vol. 2, p. 207.

11 Anthony Netboy, *The Columbia River Salmon and Steelhead Trout: Their Fight for Survival* (Seattle, 1980), pp. 17–18.

12 Gunther, 'Analysis of the First Salmon Ceremony', pp. 615–16. Western Europeans held first salmon ceremonies too. At the English village of Norham in Northumberland, commercial salmon fishing on the Tweed is now moribund. Yet Norham's venerable tradition of net fishing from cobbles is still commemorated on the opening night of the salmon season (14 February). The local vicar comes down to the Pedwell fishery at midnight and blesses the nets. In return, he receives the first salmon. Nearby Tweedmouth has an annual salmon queen festival that begins the Sunday after 18 July, culminating in the coronation of the Tweedmouth Salmon Queen.

13 Takako Yamada, *The World View of the Ainu* (New York, 2001), p. 129.

14 Hitoshi Watanabe, *The Ainu Ecosystem: Environment and Group Structure* (Seattle, 1973), pp. 71–3.

15 For a 1920s account of Ainu rituals, see Ito Oda, 'Traveling by Dugout on the Chitose River and Sending the Salmon Spirits Home: Memoir of an Ainu Woman', in *First Fish, First People: Salmon Tales of the North Pacific Rim*, ed. Judith Roche and Meg McHutchinson (Seattle, 1998), pp. 123–31.

16 Roche and McHutchinson, eds, *First Fish, First People*, p. 92.

17 Georg Wilhelm Steller/Stepan Petrovich Krasheninnikov, *The History of Kamtschatka, and the Kurilski Islands, with the Countries Adjacent*, trans. James Grieve (Gloucester, 1764), p. 146.

18 Isabella Augusta (Lady) Gregory, *Gods and Fighting Men* (London, 1904), p. 162.

19 Martin Martin, *Description of the Western Islands of Scotland* (London, 1703), p. 7.

20 Robert B. K. Stevenson, 'The Inchyra Stone and Some Other Unpublished Early Christian Monuments', *Proceedings of the Society of Scottish Antiquaries* (1958–9), pp. 33–6.

21 Kathryn McKay and Anne Ikeda, 'Unpacking the Label: British Columbian Salmon Can Imagery in the 20th Century', in *Trademarks and Salmon Art: A Brand New Perspective*, ed. Anne Ikeda and Kathi Lees (Richmond, BC, 2002), pp. 33–6.

22 Ibid., p. 37.

23 Decimus Magnus Ausonius, *The Mosella*, trans. E. H. Blakeney (London, 1933), lines 9–11. Salmon have been absent from the Mosel since the 1880s.

24 Seamus Heaney, *Door into the Dark* (London, 1969), p. 18.

25 Tim Bowling, *Low Water Slack* (Gibsons, BC, 1995), p. 33.

26 Sherman Alexie, *The Man Who Loves Salmon* (Boise, ID, 1998).

27 Ted Hughes, *River* (London, 1983), pp. 8, 18, 64, 98, 112, 114.

28 Tom Pero, '"So Quickly It's Over": An Interview with Ted Hughes', *Wild Steelhead and Salmon Magazine*, 5/2 (Winter 1999), pp. 50–58.

29 Brenda Colloms, *Charles Kingsley: The Lion of Eversley* (London, 1975), p. 256.

30 Charles Kingsley, *The Water-Babies: A Fairy Tale for a Land-Baby* (London, 1901 [1863]), pp. 106–8, 122–6.

31 Williamson closely monitored the portrayal of Salar's anatomical features by his illustrator, Charles F. Tunnicliffe; see Ian Niall, *Portrait of a Country Artist: C. F. Tunnicliffe, R.A., 1901–1979* (London, 1980), pp. 73, 76.

32 Henry Williamson, *Salar the Salmon* (New York, 1965 [1935]), pp. 14, 37, 12, 43, 131, 185.

33 Neil Gunn, *Highland River* (Edinburgh, 1937), pp. 11, 16, 168, 203, 320, 304, 330–31.

34 Boria Sax, H-NILAS (Nature in Legend and Story), online discussion list, 8 June 1997, http://www.h-net.org/~nilas/.

35 Johani's most ambitious plan, inspired by the 3,000-year-old Uffington White Horse on Berkshire's chalk downlands (now part of Oxfordshire), is to carve a 150-metre salmon into a bare hillside above Port Townsend's airport.

36 As quoted in Deborah Woolston, 'Salmon Take to the Streets',
    Bremerton Sun, 17 November 2001. Soul Salmon itself was inspired
    by a Chicago project involving cow sculptures.

37 Online at http://www.soulsalmon.org.

38 Online at http://www.salmonnation.com/declaration/Dec_Inter
    dependence.cfm. You can taste Salmon Nation at Vancouver
    International Airport, where gift shops sell salmon candy
    (smoked salmon coated in maple syrup and studded with pepper-
    corns) and pink bubble gum in the form of salmon eggs.

39 Since it opened in 1984, hundreds of thousands of schoolchildren
    have filed through the hands-on museum, scrutinizing hatching
    eggs through magnifying glasses and gazing at the different
    species in their aquariums. In spring, children can release fry into
    the Toyohira (the river that flows through the city) and in the
    autumn they watch spawning in an outdoor pool.

40 Chisato O. Dubreuil, 'Ainu-e: Instructional Resources for the Study
    of Japan's Other People', *Education About Asia*, 9/1 (Spring 2004),
    p. 10. Ainu-e is a genre of Japanese painting depicting Ainu lives.

41 Boria Sax, H-NILAS (Nature in Legend and Story), online discus-
    sion list, 8 June 1997, http://www.h-net.org/~nilas/.

CONCLUSION

1 'New Bush Salmon Rules Spark Controversy', *Sacramento Bee*,
   3 May 2004.

2 Rik Scarce, *Fishy Business: Salmon, Biology, and the Social
   Construction of Nature* (Philadelphia, 1999), pp. 112–14.

3 Lisa Mighetto and Wesley J. Ebel, *Saving the Salmon: A History of
   the US Army Corps of Engineers' Efforts to Protect Anadromous Fish on
   the Columbia and Snake Rivers* (Seattle, 1994), p. 174.

4 Visit Salmon Nation's website and you will be urged to declare
   your citizenship by taking the Salmon Nation Oath. Once you
   have pledged allegiance, you can apply for your Salmon Nation
   Citizenship Pack – but only if you live in the US or Canada.

Bibliography

Alexie, Sherman, *The Man Who Loves Salmon* (Boise, ID, 1998)

Augerot, Xanthippe, *Atlas of Pacific Salmon: The First Map-Based Status Assessment of Salmon in the North Pacific* (Berkeley, CA, 2005)

Barinaga, Marcia, 'Salmon Follow Watery Odors Home', *Science* 286/5440 (22 October 1999), pp. 705–6.

Bilton, William, *Two Summers in Norway*, 2 vols (London, 1840)

Bowling, Tim, *Low Water Slack* (Gibsons, BC, 1995)

Buckland, Frank, *Manual of Salmon and Trout Hatching* (London, 1864)

——, 'A Salmon Caught in the Thames', *Land and Water*, 9 (23 April 1870) p. 292.

Clark, Ernest Dunbar, *The Salmon Canning Industry* (Seattle, 1927)

Davy, Humphry, *Salmonia: or Days of Fly Fishing* (London, 1828)

Dawson, Kenneth, *Salmon and Trout in Moorland Streams* (London, 1928)

Day, Francis, *British and Irish Salmonidae* (London, 1887)

Dickens, Charles, 'Salmon', *All The Year Round: A Weekly Journal*, 20 July 1861, p. 406.

Franck, Richard, *Northern Memoirs, Calculated for the Meridian of Scotland* (London, 1694)

Greenhalgh, Malcolm, *The Complete Salmon Fisher*, I: *The Life of the Salmon* (London, 1996)

Gregory, Isabella Augusta, *Gods and Fighting Men* (London, 1904)

Grimble, Augustus, *The Salmon Rivers of Scotland*, 4 vols (London, 1899–1900)

Groot, C. and L. Margolis, eds, *Pacific Salmon Life Histories* (Vancouver, BC, 1991)

Gunn, Neil. *Highland River* (Edinburgh, 1937)

Gunther, Erna, 'An Analysis of the First Salmon Ceremony', *American Anthropologist*, 28/4 (1926), pp. 605–17

Haig-Brown, Roderick Langmere, *Return to the River: A Story of the Chinook Run* (New York, 1941)

Hallock, Charles, *The Salmon Fisher* (New York, 1890)

Hasler, Arthur, *Underwater Guideposts: Homing of Salmon* (Madison, WI, 1966)

Heaney, Seamus, *Door into the Dark* (London, 1969)

Hughes, Ted, *River* (London, 1983)

Hume, R. D., *Salmon of the Pacific Coast* (San Francisco, 1893)

Humphrys, John, *The Great Food Gamble* (London, 2001)

Hutton, J. Arthur, *The Life-History of the Salmon* (Aberdeen, 1924)

Ikeda, Anne and Kathi Lees, eds, *Trademarks and Salmon Art: A Brand New Perspective* (Richmond, BC, 2002)

Jardine, William, *Illustrations of British Salmonidae with Descriptions by Sir William Jardine* (Edinburgh, 1839–41),

Jones, J. W., *The Salmon* (London, 1959)

Kingsley, Charles, *The Water-Babies: A Fairy Tale for a Land-Baby* (London, 1863)

Kipling, Rudyard, *From Sea to Sea and Other Sketches: Letters of Travel*, 2 vols (London, 1904)

Kurlansky, Mark, *Cod: A Biography of the Fish That Changed the World* (London, 1998)

Lang, William, 'Beavers, Firs, Salmon, and Falling Water: Pacific Northwest Regionalism and the Environment', *Oregon Historical Quarterly*, 104/2 (Summer 2003), pp. 151–65

Lewis, Meriwether and William Clark, *The Journals of Lewis and Clark*, ed. Bernard De Voto (Boston, 1997)

Lichatowich, Jim, *Salmon Without Rivers: A History of the Pacific Salmon Crisis* (Washington, DC, 1999)

——, and Seth Zuckerman, *Salmon Nation: People, Fish, and our Common Home* (Portland, OR, 1999)

Lloyd, Lewis, *Field Sports of the North of Europe: A Narrative of Angling, Hunting and Shooting in Sweden and Norway* (London, 1885)

Malloch, P.D.H., *Life History of the Salmon, Trout and Other Freshwater Fish* (London, 1912)

Maree, Bill, *Fishing with the Presidents* (Mechanicsburg, PA, 1999)

Mawle, G. W. and N. J. Milner, 'The Return of Salmon to Cleaner Rivers – England and Wales', in Derek Mills, ed., *Salmon at the Edge* (Oxford, 2003), pp. 186–99

Menzies, W.J.M., *The Salmon: Its Life Story* (Edinburgh, 1925)

Mighetto, Lisa and Wesley J. Ebel, *Saving the Salmon: A History of the US Army Corps of Engineers' Efforts to Protect Anadromous Fish on the Columbia and Snake Rivers* (Seattle, 1994)

Moule, Thomas, *The Heraldry of Fish* (London, 1842)

Netboy, Anthony, *The Atlantic Salmon: A Vanishing Species?* (London, 1968)

——, *The Columbia River Salmon and Steelhead Trout: Their Fight for Survival* (Seattle, 1980)

Parenteau, Bill, 'A "Very Determined Opposition to the Law": Conservation, Angling Leases, and Social Conflict in the Canadian Atlantic Salmon Fishery, 1867–1914', *Environmental History*, 9 (July 2004). pp. 436–63

Phair, Charles, *Atlantic Salmon Fishing*, 2 vols (New York, 1937)

Roche, Judith and Meg McHutchison, eds, *First Fish, First People: Salmon Tales of the North Pacific Rim* (Seattle, 1998)

Russel, Alexander, *The Salmon* (Edinburgh, 1864)

Scott, Walter, *Guy Mannering* (Edinburgh, 1815)

——, *The Tale of Old Mortality* (Edinburgh, 1816)

——, *Redgauntlet* (Edinburgh, 1824)

Scrope, William, *Days and Nights of Salmon Fishing in the Tweed* (London, 1843)

Shearer, W. M., *The Atlantic Salmon: Natural History, Exploitation and Future Management* (Oxford, 1992)

Steller, Georg Wilhelm and Stepan Petrovich Krasheninnikov, *The History of Kamtschatka, and the Kurilski Islands, with the Countries Adjacent*, trans. James Grieve (Gloucester, 1764)

Stoddart, Thomas Tod, *The Art of Angling as Practised in Scotland* (Edinburgh, 1835)

——, *The Angler's Companion to the Rivers and Lochs of Scotland* (Edinburgh, 1847)

Taylor, Joseph E. III, 'El Niño and Vanishing Salmon: Culture, Nature, History, and the Politics of Blame', *Western Historical Quarterly*, 29 (Winter 1998), pp. 437–57

——, *Making Salmon: An Environmental History of the Northwest Fisheries Crisis* (Seattle, 1999)

——, 'Regional Unifier or Social Catspaw? A Social and Cultural Historical Geography of Salmon Recovery', in *Imagining the Big Open: Nature, Identity, and Play in the New West*, ed. Liza Nicholas et al (Salt Lake City, 2003), pp. 3–26

Tchernavin, V., 'The Origin of Salmon, Its Ancestry Marine or Freshwater?', *Salmon and Trout Magazine*, 95 (1939), pp. 120–40

Tolfrey, Frederic, *Jones's Guide to Norway, and Salmon Fisher's Pocket Companion* (London, 1848)

Ulrich, Roberta, *Empty Nets: Indians, Dams, and the Columbia River* (Corvallis, OR, 1999)

Williamson, Henry, *Salar the Salmon* (London, 1935)

Yarrell, William, 'The Salmon', in *A History of British Fishes*, 2 vols (London, 1836)

Associations and Websites

Atlantic Salmon Federation
St Andrews, New Brunswick, Canada / Calais, Maine, USA, has one of the most comprehensive online collections of information, including a guide to the Atlantic Salmon Conservation Centre:
http://www.asf.ca/

Atlantic Salmon Trust
Pitlochry, Scotland, funds and conducts research into the problems that confront wild Atlantic salmon and sea trout; it has a website with a particularly useful section called 'Salmon Facts':
http://www.atlanticsalmontrust.org

Salmons Webpage
in French, German and English maintained by RiverNet is the best source of information about the current and recent situation of the Atlantic salmon in continental western Europe:
http://www.rivernet.org/general/salmon/saumo.e.htm

Wild Salmon Center
an organization based at Portland, Oregon (with Russian offices in Moscow and Elisovo, Kamchatka), dedicated to the scientific understanding and protection of the finest remaining ecosystems of salmon in the North Pacific:
http://www.wildsalmoncenter.org.

State of the Salmon
site maintained by the Wild Salmon Center and Ecotrust, the most up-to-date guide to the condition, distribution and management

of the various species of *Oncorhynchus*:
http://www.stateofthesalmon.org

The Salmon Page

hosted by Riverdale Grade School in Portland, Oregon ('all things salmon: catch them, cook them, save them'), is a gateway to a huge number of salmon-related sites:
http://www.riverdale.k12.or.us/salmon.htm.

Salmon Nation

the ultimate website for lovers of salmon on North America's Pacific coast who wish to live in a salmon-friendly manner:
http://www.salmonnation.com/.

The Salmon Farm Monitor

maintained by the Scottish-based Salmon Farm Protest Group, provides extensive coverage of the case against farmed salmon, including a bulky archive:
http://www.salmonfarmmonitor.org

Scottish Quality Salmon

an industry organization, puts the case for sustainable, environmentally responsible salmon farming that also takes fish welfare seriously:
http://www.scottishsalmon.co.uk.

GoldSeal

the leading brand of the Canadian Fishing Company (Canfisco), has a 'Wild Salmon Spotlight' with information about life history, West Coast canning, and conservation efforts:
http://www.goldseal.ca/wildsalmon/

Salmon skin leather haute couture

for the latest, from bikinis to sandals, visit the website of SKINI London: http://www.skinilondon.com

Acknowledgements

My two teenage daughters have ribbed me mercilessly during the writing of this book. I've cheerfully weathered routine comments such as 'Dad, who, apart from your seriously weird friends, is going to buy this book?' and 'How come you aren't having salmon for breakfast this morning?' One day, clearly worried that my salmon obsession had gone too far, Ivana (who insisted I should have been writing about a fish that was actually interesting – such as the piranha) asked me whether I'd rather be a salmon or a person. My reply to this profound question ('Surely you already know the answer to that') did nothing to reassure her. On another occasion, when particularly annoyed with me, she told one of her friends in a bitter tone that her father probably wished that he'd had salmon instead of children. Yet one of the sweetest things that Giuliana has said to me recently is that when she's rich and famous she'll buy me my own river that I can fill with as many salmon as I like. (I shall remind her of this promise in years to come.) But this one is for Graziella – not least for first spotting flash-frozen crimson-coloured wild Alaska sockeye salmon at the supermarket fish counter.

I'd also like to thank the following for various forms of assistance or simply for being so keen to talk salmon with me: Will Adams, Johnny Ajluni, Jeremy Bristow, Jonathan Burt, Jess Dunton, Claudia Escobar, Simon Evans, Richard Harrad, Ron Inouye, Susan Irby, Joe Jissel, Sara Mall Johani, Seth Johnson-Marshall, Mike Johnston, 'Pete River' Kaufman, Gideon Lack, Harry Marshall, Garry Marvin (for bringing the 'Animal' series to my attention), Tom Moffatt, Heather Pegg, Gabrielle Rivers, Stephen Marsh-Smith, Steve Wells and Adrian Williams. I also wish to acknowledge the enormous assistance that the University of Bristol provided in the shape of a University Research Fellowship, without which this book could never have been completed in timely fashion. My university's Arts Faculty Research Fund and BIRTHA Institute also contributed to the cost of reproducing the illustrations.

Photo Acknowledgements

The author and publishers wish to express their thanks to the below sources of illustrative material and/or permission to reproduce it. (Some sources uncredited in the captions for reasons of brevity are also given below.)

Photo American Philosophical Society, Philadelphia: p. 61; illustration © Atlantic Salmon Federation: p. 22 (artwork, J. O. Pennanen); photos courtesy of the Atlantic Salmon Trust and the A. K. Bell Library, Perth and Kinross Council, Scotland: pp. 118, 127; photo author: p. 145 (top); photo © Todd Bingham/2006 iStock International Inc.: p. 126; Bodleian Library, Oxford (photos Oxford University Libraries Imaging Services, © Bodleian Library, University of Oxford): pp. 15 (Shelfmark Tab.N.2. Douce W. subt. 84), 28 foot (Shelfmark 18953e.71, Plate 98); photos British Columbia Archives, Royal British Columbia Museum, Victoria, BC, Canada: pp. 36, 157 (foot), 158 (top); British Library, London (photo courtesy of the British Library): p. 65; illustrations courtesy of the Canadian Fishing Company (Gold Seal Seafoods): p. 159 (lower left and lower right); photo Ian B. Dearing, Clitheroe, Lancs: p. 115; illustrations by Shari Erickson: p. 17, 18, 19, 20; from Charles Hallock, *The Salmon Fisher* (New York, 1890): p. 130; photo International News Photos, Inc.: p. 137; photo © The Bikini Chef Susan Irby: p. 82; photo courtesy of Sergey Ivanov, Stamprussia.com: p. 145 (middle right); photos courtesy of Sara Mall Johani: pp. 170, 171; photo curtesy of The Judge's Lodging Museum, Presteigne, Wales: p. 120; photos from the Laboratory for Vertebrate Paleontology, University of Alberta, British Columbia, courtesy of Dr Mark H. Wilson: p. 14; photo Lady Lever Art Gallery, National Museums Liverpool: p. 135; photos Library of Congress, Washington, DC: pp. 24 (photo Lillie N. Gordon, Frank and Frances Carpenter Collection, LOT 11453-1, no. 139), 57 (Prints and Photographs Division, Edward Curtis Collection, LC-USZ62-113079), 63 top (Prints and Photographs Division, LC-USZ62-114925), 63 foot (Prints and Photographs Division, Frank and Frances Carpenter Collection, LOT 11453-1, no. 195), 64 (Prints and Photographs Division, LC-USZ62-72025), 66 (Prints and Photographs Division, LC-USZ62-95113), 72 (bottom left) (Prints and Photographs Division, Farm Security Administration/Office of War Information Photograph Collection, LC-USF34-070312-D), 72 (bottom right) (Prints and Photographs Division, Farm Security Administration/Office of War Information Photograph Collection, LC-USF34-070457-D), 73 right (Frank and Frances Carpenter Collection, Prints and Photographs Division, Library of Congress

(LOT 11453-1, no. 734), 74 (Prints and Photographs Division, Farm Security Administration/Office of War Information Photograph Collection, LC-USF33-013149-M4), 89 (Division of Prints and Photographs, Farm Security Administration/Office of War Information Photograph Collection, LC-USF33-013150-M1), 91 (Prints and Photographs Division, Farm Security Administration/Office of War Information Collection, LC-USF34-070672-D), 93 (top left) (Prints and Photographs Division, Farm Security Administration/Office of War Information Collection, LC-USW33-05416-C), 114 (Division of Prints and Photographs, Frank and Frances Carpenter collection, LOT 11453-1, no. 75); from Lewis Lloyd, *Scandinavian Adventures* (London, 1854): p. 134; photo courtesy of Kate Hedges and the Maidu tribe (Kontow Valley Band, Oroville, California): p. 151; photo Pedro Marinello/SKINI London, courtesy of Claudia Escobar: p. 83; photo © Stefan Meyers: p. 54; from Thomas Moule, *Heraldry of Fish: Notices of the Principal Families Bearing Fish in their Arms* (London, 1842): pp. 146 (top left and right); photo courtesy of the Museum of History & Industry, Seattle: p. 122 (from the *Seattle Post-Intelligencer*, 2 March 1964); photo The National Archives, Kew: p. 112; photos courtesy of Oregon State Archives, Salem: pp. 93 top right (Oregon Department of Transportation) 95 (Water Resources Department), 125 top (Oregon Department of Fish and Wildlife); photos Perth Museum and Art Gallery, Perth and Kinross Council, Scotland: pp. 139, 157 (top); illustration reproduced by kind permission of *Private Eye*/Mark Barfield: p. 99; photos courtesy of The Queens College Library, University of Oxford (© of the Provost, Fellows and Scholars of the Queens College, Oxford): pp. 42, 43; Radnorshire Museum, Llandrindod Wells, Wales: pp. 119, 125 (foot), 129, 132; photo Rex Features/Sipa Press: p. 6 (244834B); photo Robert W. Richmond: p. 169; photo Alain Roussot: p. 156; photos Lee Russell: pp. 89, 91; photo Charles Sainsbury-Plaice (Agripix Ltd): p. 81; Shelburne Museum, Vermont: p. 160 (photo Shelburne Museum); illustrations © C. F. Tunnicliffe Estate: p. 168; photo University of Bristol Arts and Social Sciences Library: p. 73 (left); photos University of Bristol Photographic Unit: pp. 21 (from Jonathan Couch's 4-vol. *A History of the Fishes of the British Islands*, 1860–65), 28 (top) (from Francis Day, *British and Irish Salmonidæ*, London, 1887), 32, 34, 35 (all from P. D. Malloch, *Life-History and Habits of the Salmon, Sea-Trout, Trout, and Other Freshwater Fish*, 1912), 40 (top) (from Frank Buckland, *Manual of Salmon and Trout Hatching*, 1864), 73 (left), 166 (from Charles Kingsley, *The Water-Babies*, 1863); photo courtesy of the University of Leiden library, Netherlands: p. 60; photos US Fish and Wildlife Service: pp. 26, 39, 40 (foot); photo VintageFish, Sausalito, California: p. 145 (lower right); photos courtesy of John West Foods, Liverpool: p. 72 (top), 75, 158 (foot), 159 (top); photo courtesy of Adrian Williams, Goldcliff Fisheries: p. 113; photos courtesy of Anne Williamson, Henry Williamson Society: pp. 167, 168; courtesy of the Wye & Usk Foundation: pp. 29, 142 (photo Seth Johnson-Marshall).

Index

215